Taking Flight

My Story by Vicki Van Meter

with Dan Gutman

VIKING

VIKING
Published by the Penguin Group
Penguin Books USA Inc., 375 Hudson Street, New York, New York 10014, U.S.A.
Penguin Books Ltd, 27 Wrights Lane, London W8 5TZ, England
Penguin Books Australia Ltd, Ringwood, Victoria, Australia
Penguin Books Canada Ltd, 10 Alcorn Avenue, Toronto, Ontario, Canada M4V 3B2
Penguin Books (N.Z.) Ltd, 182–190 Wairau Road, Auckland 10, New Zealand

Penguin Books Ltd, Registered Offices: Harmondsworth, Middlesex, England

First published in 1995 by Viking, a division of Penguin Books USA Inc.

1   3   5   7   9   10   8   6   4   2

Most photos which appear in the book were provided by the Van Meter family, with the following exceptions:
Photos on pages 2, 9, and 130 by Kevin Foster
Photo on page 15 by Dan Gutman
Photos on pages 26, 57, 78, 98 and 121 courtesy of The Associated Press
Maps created by Nina Wallace

LIBRARY OF CONGRESS CATALOGING-IN-PUBLICATION DATA
Van Meter, Vicki.
Taking flight : my story / by Vicki Van Meter, with Dan Gutman.   p.   cm.
ISBN 0-670-86260-6
1. Van Meter, Vicki—Juvenile literature. 2. Children as air pilots—United States—Biography—Juvenile literature.
3. Women air pilots—United States—Biography—Juvenile literature. [1. Van Meter, Vicki. 2. Air Pilots.
3. Women—Biography. 4. Children's writings.] I. Gutman, Dan. II. Title.
TL540.V323A3 1995 629.13'092—dc20 [B] 94-44067 CIP AC

Printed in U.S.A.
Set in Perpetua

To my mom and dad and brother and sister,
who always stuck by me and gave me support.

"I want to do it because I must do it.
Women must try to do things as men have tried.
When they fail, their failure must be a
challenge to others."

—Amelia Earhart, 1937

Contents

Contents

Acknowledgments

During my flights across the country and across the Atlantic Ocean, some people said there was no way a girl my age could have done these things by herself. They were right. A lot of people helped me along the way:

Curt Arnspiger, my co-pilot, whose willingness to work with me and whose patience and positive attitude helped me get across the Atlantic. Bob Baumgartner, who believed in me and taught me how to fly. Diane Dowler and Marie Rozakis, my sixth grade teachers who helped me get my work done and always understood. Stan Parkins, who helped me more than he'll ever know. Linda Pitts, for being my buddy. Mike Riley and Dick Willis, who shared their time and knowledge with me. Bob Robbins, who has always been there for me. Peter Thompson, for his enthusiasm, vision, and friendship. Morris Waid, a fellow pilot who always supported me. The kids in my class at East End Elementary School, who accepted my interest in flying and encouraged me every step of the way. Grammy, all my aunts, uncles, and cousins, who mean so much to me. And all those known and unknown people who offered their kindness or prayers. I couldn't have done what I did without you.

But I did all the flying *myself*.

As far back as I can remember, I wanted to be an astronaut.

When I was a little girl I was interested in the planets, stars, UFOs, and things like that. As I grew up, I became fascinated with the idea of actually visiting outer space, of going somewhere only a few human beings had ever gone before. I wanted to experience something that hardly anyone on our planet had experienced.

I never thought about flying a "plain old plane."

But one morning my dad read in the newspaper that a new terminal building was being dedicated at our local airport. He asked me if I wanted to go see it. I had nothing better to do that day, so I went along for the ride.

At the airport, we noticed a sign-up sheet for people interested in taking a flying lesson.

"If you want to fly to Mars someday," my dad said, "maybe you should see what flying is like."

Okay, I thought, I'll take a lesson. My dad asked at the desk if ten-year-olds were allowed to take the flying lesson, and he was told that there was no age restriction—all students fly with an instructor. Dad added my name to the list and we left.

That was September 27, 1992. At that time, my idea of a big trip was to drive with my family to the mall thirty-five miles away in Erie, Pennsylvania. If you had told me that in the next year and a half I would pilot a plane across the United States, over the Atlantic Ocean, survive two midair emergencies, appear on *The Tonight Show*, tour the White House, and be recognized by strangers on the street from New York to Iceland, I would have said you were out of your mind.

But that's exactly what happened.

—Vicki Van Meter, 1995

This is the Cessna 172 that would take me from Maine to California.

1

"There was this look of power in her face."

I live in Meadville, Pennsylvania. It's a small town of 14,000 people in Crawford County, about ninety miles north of Pittsburgh.

New York City is famous for its skyscrapers. Los Angeles is famous for its movie stars. Meadville is famous too—in 1913 the first zipper was manufactured in Meadville. In fact, the man who made it, Colonel Lewis Walker, lived in the house right across the street from mine.

I was born on March 13, 1982. When I'm not flying, I collect stuffed animals, trolls, pigs, keychains, and baseball cards. I like to play baseball, basketball, tennis—just about any sport really.

I've taken violin lessons but I didn't enjoy them very much so I never practiced. That's probably because my favorite music is heavy metal—Metallica, Green Day, Aerosmith, Pearl Jam, that kind of stuff. Now I think I want to learn how to play the drums.

Me and my stuff.

I'm a good student, and my favorite subjects are math, science, and social studies.

My brother Daniel is three years older than me, and my sister Elizabeth is four years older than Daniel. We all fight, and we all love each other.

2

Vicki's Brother Daniel

"When we were younger we used to take trips to my grand-mother's house in Ohio. The Rocky *movies were pretty big back then. The trips were pretty boring. There was a big bed in the back of the van and we'd play 'Rock Fighter.' I'd be Vicki's coach and she'd wrestle against Liz. Liz was much bigger and she could have sat on Vicki if she wanted to, but that never stopped Vicki from trying to beat Liz. She'd get really mad if she didn't win. I'd jump in there every once in a while too. Things got out of hand sometimes and my dad would have to pull over to the side of the road until we calmed down."*

When my dad signed me up for that flying lesson, I didn't think much of it. We didn't bother mentioning it to my mom when we got home. I never even thought the flight school would call.

But a few days later the phone rang and my mom picked it up. The man at the other end of the line told her my first flying lesson was scheduled for Thursday.

"Her first *what?!*" she exclaimed.

My mom didn't come to the airport for my first flying lesson. She said she had errands to run, but I knew she was too nervous to watch me get into a small airplane and fly off. She gets nervous pretty easily. My dad drove me over to

The inside of a single engine plane is smaller than a compact car. It gets really cramped in there after a few hours.

the Port Meadville Airport. We were introduced to the instructor, Bob Baumgartner.

He seemed like a tough, no-nonsense kind of guy and he looked like he was in his forties. Bob led me over to a little plane, a Cessna 150. It's a single engine plane, with the propeller in the front. It's also a high wing plane, which means the wing sits *above* the cockpit. I sat on the left in the pilot's seat, and Bob sat on the right.

He taxied down the runway and lifted off the ground like he was pulling his car out of a driveway. I had been on plane trips before, but in a big jet you hardly even notice you're flying. The Cessna is very small and light. Every gust of wind

4

blows the plane around. And sitting up front in the cockpit was a completely new experience.

Once we were in the air, Bob showed me how the controls worked. Instead of a steering wheel, planes have a yoke—sort of like a small handlebar on a bicycle. The pilot and copilot each have a yoke, and they move together. Bob moved the yoke to the left and the plane banked to the left. Then he moved it to the right and the plane banked that way. He pulled the yoke toward him, and the Cessna started to climb. He pushed it away from him, and the nose of the plane went into a gradual dive. He showed me how the yoke moves the ailerons on the wings and the elevators on the tail to make the plane change direction.

"Go ahead," he said, taking his hands off his yoke. "Try it."

I grabbed the yoke with both hands. I turned it left a little bit and felt the plane instantly react and turn that way. I banked it right and took it up and down. It felt very natural. I didn't feel nervous at all. It was thrilling to be controlling a plane.

While I moved the yoke, Bob told me about the instrument panel. There are about twenty dials and gauges on the dashboard to give the pilot information—speed, revolutions per minute, oil pressure, oil temperature, vertical speed indicator. There's a banking indicator to tell you how many degrees the plane is tilted. The altimeter is sensitive to air pressure, and calculates how high the plane is flying. The artificial horizon helps you tell if you're climbing. And, of course, every plane has a compass.

Another gauge tells you how many hours the plane has flown. The pilot has to copy that number down every time he or she lands to know how much to pay to rent the plane.

There's a throttle, lights, heater, radio, a bunch of circuit breakers, and a parking brake. I noticed that there was no rearview mirror on the plane and that the windows didn't roll up and down.

The Cessna has two fuel gauges. Fuel is stored in tanks within the wings. Each wing holds eighteen gallons, and you can turn the tanks on and off individually. Bob explained that the pilot tries to keep the two tanks pretty even so the weight of the plane is balanced.

You can't just bring a plane to a regular gas station and tell the attendant "fill 'er up." Airplane engines use a special fuel designed to burn at higher altitudes than the gas you put in a car. It costs about two dollars a gallon.

There was no way to absorb all that information in one lesson, especially when I was having so much fun just banking left and right, soaring through the sky.

There's one more dial on the dashboard—a clock. It seemed we had only been in the air for a few minutes, but an hour had flown by (in more ways than one!). Bob took over the controls and swooped down, landing smoothly on the same runway we started from. He used the two rudder pedals on the floor to steer.

I was disappointed that the lesson was over. Flying the plane had given me sort of a tingling sensation all over. I had discovered something that I enjoyed more than anything else I'd ever experienced.

Vicki's Mother Corinne

"I was too nervous to watch her take off, but I wanted to be there at the end of the lesson. When she got out of the plane and walked toward me, there was this look of power in her face. She had really found a challenge she could sink her teeth into. I knew from her first flight that this was not going to be just a passing fancy."

People ask me why I like to fly, and that's the hardest question for me to answer. For most people, I realize, flying in a plane is just a way to get from one place to another. For me, it's something more than that.

Being in control of a plane and being able to fly it wherever I want makes me feel free. From the cockpit of a small plane, you can see a view that most people never get to experience. One time I saw a horse race from above, and it was so strange to look at it from that angle.

I'm not very good at explaining things like this. Some people enjoy being artists but don't know why. They just like to paint. I just like to fly.

The funny thing is, I'm afraid of heights. When I'm in a tall building, I can't stand too close to the windows. I know it's perfectly safe, but I still have a funny feeling about it. In a plane, it's different. In a plane, I'm in control. I know I'm not going to fall.

Maybe flying is in my genes. My grandfather, who died before I was born, was an air traffic controller. He met my grandmother when she was working with the United States Weather Bureau. My father was also a pilot. He owned a Piper Tri-Pacer when he was younger, but when he met my mother, he sold it to help put her through college. He hasn't flown in thirty years.

Vicki's Friend Kevin Carlson

"I was sitting in social studies class one day. Vicki was in the seat in front of me and she turned around and whispered, 'Hey, Kevin, guess what I did yesterday?'

'What?' I said.

'I flew an airplane.'

'Get outta here!' I scoffed. I really didn't know if she was telling the truth or not."

At my second flying lesson, Bob let me take the plane off the ground. At my third, he let me help him land it. By that time, I had made a decision. I didn't have to break the news to my parents. We all knew that I had decided I was going to become a pilot.

My brother Daniel, our friend Luke, and my sister Elizabeth taking a break from shooting hoops.

Vicki's Mother Corinne

"She taught me very early in life that she was going to do what she wanted. I remember one time Vicki was three years old

and I took her to buy pants. She hated frilly, fashionable clothes, insisting on plain straight-legged jeans. I found a pair of pants I liked and convinced her to at least try it on. She did, and I told her how nice she looked. She said she preferred the plain blue jeans.

'We don't have to buy anything right now,' I told her. 'Let's come back another day.'

She looked at me and she said, 'Mom, whose decision is this?' "

2

"Nice landing for a kid!"

To become a pilot, you don't just get in a plane and learn how to fly. It's more like getting a driver's license. First you have to pass a written test. To do that, you have to go to ground school.

Over the next ten weeks, I spent thirty hours in a room with ten adults learning the ins and outs of piloting a plane. For some reason, nearly all of the other students were smokers. I have some allergies, and the cigarette smoke really bothered my sinuses.

To attend ground school, I had to miss my basketball season at school, and I really wanted to play. That made me

My first flight instructor, Bob Baumgartner. The woman on my left is Theresa Brown, our state representative.

pretty upset, but I guess I wanted to fly more than I wanted to play basketball.

Before the first lesson, Bob got up in front of the class and told us to tell everyone our name and what we do for a living. The first guy said, "I'm Joe and I'm a dairy farmer." A woman got up and said, "I'm an accountant." It went around like that. I felt a little bit out of place and nervous because I didn't know what to say.

Finally it was my turn. I stood up and said, "My name is Vicki. I'm in the fifth grade at East End School and I like to play baseball."

Everybody laughed. It didn't bother them that there was a ten-year-old kid in the class, and they were all really nice to me.

Each class, one of us would bring a few dozen doughnuts and we'd take a break in the middle of the session to eat them. I would use the fifteen-minute break time to do my regular schoolwork.

One night, I was eating a coconut doughnut and studying for my science exam when this guy Bob Swanson suddenly shouted, "Hey! Somebody took my coconut doughnut!" He looked at me and said, "It was *you!*"

After that, he would always accuse me of stealing his doughnuts, and I would accuse him of stealing mine.

Ground school was pretty boring. I wanted to get off the ground and start flying. Sitting in the classroom, I found it hard to understand what I was learning about piloting a plane. We had to sit through these awful movies where they'd try and be funny by saying stuff like "Don't fly into the trees." They weren't funny at all.

Bob gave us homework too. We had to answer ten questions based on those awful movies we watched in class. I was used to doing homework from school, but I guess the rest of the class hadn't been assigned homework in years. When we showed up for the second class, Bob asked everyone to turn in their homework, and I was the only one who had done it!

Going to ground school and regular school at the same time was really hard. When the ten weeks finally were over, Bob gave us our written test. It had fifty questions. I remember one of them was "How do you know you're on a direct course with another aircraft?" The answer is that it looks like the plane coming toward you isn't moving at all.

I only got about half the answers right and was devastated when I found out I had failed the test. But I really wanted to become a pilot more than anything in the world. I signed up for the class *again*, and did the whole ten week course a second time.

This time I got a 98, and passed with "flying colors."

The F.A.A. (the Federal Aviation Administration) prohibits anyone under the age of sixteen from getting a pilot's license or flying a plane solo. I would have to wait six years for that. But I had passed the written test and I could pilot a plane all by myself as long as an instructor was sitting next to me.

I could fly, and that was all that mattered.

When you sit down in a plane's cockpit, there are a whole series of things you have to do before you take off. You have to start the ignition, of course. It's important to move all the controls so that you know they're working. You have to turn the radio on and communicate with the air traffic controller.

The instrument panel of the Cessna 172. It looks pretty complicated, but it's not that hard to learn. That gizmo attached to the yoke is a plain old calculator.

You don't just pick up the handset and say, "Hey buddy, it's me Vicki and I'm taking off." It's important for the controller to clear a runway for your plane, and to make certain that none of the other pilots in the area try to take off or land on that runway at the same time you're taking off.

To make sure pilots and controllers understand each other perfectly, there's a standard alphabet for aviation. When you need to say the letter A, you say "alpha." You say "bravo" for B, "charley" for C, and so on until you get to Z ("zulu"). And each plane has a code, such as 8802U. Whenever anybody says anything to you over the radio, you're supposed to repeat it back to them to let them know that you understood what they said.

For me, radio communication is the hardest part about flying. Even with the alphabet, it's difficult to understand what people are saying. There's often a lot of static. I don't do much chatting while I'm flying.

Here's how a takeoff works: You receive permission to use a certain runway. You look around to make double sure there are no other planes nearby. You roll out to the runway and backtaxi to where it begins. The reason you backtaxi is so you can have as much room as possible to take off.

You line yourself up on the runway. Push the throttle all the way in. The engine roars, the propeller grabs the air, and the plane starts slowly building up speed. You use your rudder pedals to stay in a straight line on the runway. When I was learning to fly I was shorter than I am now, and it was hard to reach the pedals. My solution was to wear a pair of my sister Elizabeth's shoes. I looked really stupid, but it worked.

When you reach about seventy-five miles per hour, the plane starts shaking a little. You gradually pull the yoke toward you. That moves the elevator on the tail of the plane, and it eases the nose up off the runway. You keep on pulling the yoke toward you, and the plane gently lifts off the ground. Something about *making* that happen gives the take-off a different feeling from when you are just a passenger.

Landing the plane is probably the most important part of flying. After all, it is sort of like crashing as gently as possible.

As you approach the airport, you use the ailerons to line the plane up with the runway. At 500 feet, you do a "GUMP" check—gas, undercarriage, mixture, propeller.

Single-engine planes cruise around 150 miles an hour—you have to slow yourself down *fast* when you land. To do this, you cut back on the throttle and gradually put your flaps down. This is called "adding flaps." It will slow you down to 60 or 65 miles an hour.

You have to use your judgment here. If you find you're coming in a little short of the runway, you put your throttle in to speed up. If you're too high and it looks like you might overshoot the runway, you use the flaps earlier. If you're way off track, you don't try to make a correction. It's better to just come around again and start over.

You want to come down to the runway level, and when you're five to ten feet off the ground, flare the nose upward just a little. That way, you'll touch the back wheels down *first*, and then gently set the nose of the plane down.

One thing I really like to do is "touch and go." That's when you bring the plane down for a landing, roll on the runway for a moment or two, and then fly off again.

Sometimes in bad weather, you can't see the runway until the last instant when you pop through the clouds. That's sort of fun. But at least once I've had to come down through the rain on an airfield that had no landing lights. I was going about eighty miles an hour a few feet off the ground and I couldn't see. That was a pretty hairy one.

You hope you never have to make one, but all pilots have to practice emergency landings. If the engine suddenly quits, you would have to figure out a way to land the plane safely.

When I fly, I'm constantly looking down at the ground for empty fields and roads. There's a grass runway strip called Rust Field near my home that's fun to land on. You have to be careful, though, because you could easily get your wheels stuck in the mud on an unpaved runway.

One of the first times I practiced an emergency landing, Bob picked a field with a bunch of cows and horses in it. I didn't want to land there, but he told me to bring the plane down lower and lower. We got down to a couple of feet off the ground, and the cows were mooing and running for their lives.

Finally, just before we would have touched down, Bob told me to bring it up. Then he turned to me and said, "We could have made it."

One thing I really did *not* like to practice was stalls, which is when you slow the airspeed of the plane to the point where it stops flying. The nose on the plane starts heading down and you go into a sudden drop. Even when you know it's coming, it's a real shock to the stomach.

Hopefully, you'll never encounter these situations unexpectedly. But if you practice them, you'll be ready. I heard about a guy whose engine quit on him last year and he didn't know what to do. The plane crashed and he died.

Once I got the hang of it, I began to fly once a week. First I flew over my own house, which was pretty neat. Then I began making local trips to Erie and to Latrobe, Pennsylvania, where my godmother Alice lives. I found that I really enjoyed setting goals and achieving them. Soon I was flying to Pittsburgh and Youngstown, Ohio to visit my cousins Paula and Kara and my aunt Louise.

One time I was landing at Pittsburgh and there was a big DC-9 jet right behind me. The air traffic controller gave the DC-9 permission to land, and then he realized it would crush us because it goes much faster. I taxied as fast as I could to get out of the way. Even so, the controller had to tell the DC-9 to go around and make his approach to landing all over again. Bob told me it probably cost $500 in fuel for the DC-9 to do it again.

The air traffic controllers were usually shocked when

they found out I was piloting the plane. Once, I was talking over the radio with a controller and it didn't occur to him until after I touched down on the runway that my voice was higher than the average pilot's.

"Hey," he said, sort of flustered, "how *old* are you?"

"Ten," I replied.

"Oh my God! Is there anyone else in the plane with you?!"

"Yes," I informed him. "My instructor."

"Well who's flying the plane?"

"I am."

He paused for a moment or two, and then he said, "Nice landing for a kid!"

Vicki's Mother Corinne

"She flew up to Bangor, Maine, one night and the weather got really bad. Thunder, lightning, storms, rain. My husband said there's no way she would try to land under those conditions. She'd have to go to another airport.

It was 9:30 p.m. and I'm thinking my child is up there in the air someplace. Then it was 10:00 and we hadn't heard from her. At 10:15 the phone rings and it's Vicki.

'Hi mom!' she said. 'It was sooo neat! The lightning was lighting up the whole sky and it was the brightest I had ever seen. We were rocking and bouncing and it was sooo cool!'

*I decided right then that I couldn't be afraid for her. You
reach a point where you realize a child's life is her own."*

In March, I turned eleven. My sister Elizabeth was about to
graduate from high school. She's an actress, and she was at-
tending the North Carolina School of the Arts in Winston-
Salem.

My flights were becoming more and more ambitious, and
I decided my next goal would be to fly the 400 miles to
Elizabeth's graduation.

From the beginning, my parents had supported my flying.
They never pushed me into it but they never discouraged
me either. They paid for my lessons and other expenses,
drove me to classes, and spent a lot of time and energy to
help me become a pilot. It was the same with Elizabeth.
They saw that she really wanted to become an actress, and
they supported her. When I asked them if I could fly to Elizabeth's graduation, they gave me their okay.

The plan was for them to drive down in advance and
meet me at the airport. My instructor Bob agreed to accompany me on the flight.

This would be my first big trip. It would take four hours
to fly from Meadville to Winston-Salem.

This is probably as good a time as any for me to bring up
something kind of gross—going to the bathroom on a

plane. Single-engine planes don't *have* bathrooms. It's usually not a problem because you only fly these planes a few hours at a time. I always make it a point to use the bathroom before I take off.

Just in case of an emergency, I brought along an orange plastic container called a "Little John"—a portable toilet. I really hoped I wouldn't have to use it, especially in front of Bob.

Food is another consideration on long flights. There's not a lot of time for enjoying a leisurely meal in the air because you always have to control the plane, monitor all the gauges, and communicate with controllers and other pilots. I might bring some fruit or chips to snack on, but I don't like to take much food with me.

Also, my stomach is pretty sensitive. So I usually eat before and after a flight. I'm always pretty hungry by the time I land.

Vicki's Mother Corinne

"It was the longest trip Vicki had flown and she was late arriving. Jim and I were standing in the control tower waiting for her. The plane hadn't appeared on the radar and I was worried.

Finally it appeared on the screen. I mentioned that I would know Vicki was all right when I heard her say she was hungry. The air traffic controller heard this, and as he was giving her

*clearance to land, he added, 'Are you hungry?' There was no
answer, so he repeated it—'Are . . . you . . . hungry?'*

*Finally Vicki's voice crackled in, 'Yeah, I'm hungry.' And we
knew she was fine."*

After Elizabeth's graduation, I offered her friend Rebecca a
ride back to Meadville. She was really excited to be one of
my first passengers, but I think she expected that we would
be flying in a bigger plane. When she saw the little Cessna on
the runway, she asked, "Is that *it?*" Then she turned to my
mom and asked, "Can I drive back with you guys?" I'm not
sure if she was joking or not, but she did become my first
long distance passenger.

Vicki's Sister Elizabeth

*"I had heard about Vicki's flying but I'd been away at school
and I'd never seen her fly. It really didn't click—I couldn't
envision it. Then, when I actually saw her take off after my
graduation, I said 'Wait a minute, this is for real.' "*

All in all, the flight to and from North Carolina went just
fine. And I never had to use my "Little John."

On July 4th, Port Meadville Airport threw an air show and
I was invited to be the opening act. Three thousand people

I was the opening act at the Fourth of July air show at Port Meadville Airport. They gave me a lift back from the plane.

were there to watch the show. I performed a "short field takeoff"—instead of rolling slowly down the runway gradually building up speed, I kept the brakes on with the throttle on full. Then I released the brakes and sort of shot off into the sky.

When I landed, a Cadillac convertible was brought out to get me and I waved to the crowd as it brought me back from the runway. It was embarrassing, but, I admit, also kind of fun.

I had been flying for less than a year at that time, but I had completed more than fifty landings. Each one gave me more confidence. I felt like I was ready to take on a bigger challenge.

Vicki's Friend Sarah Abbondanza

"I was at Vicki's house one time and I saw some papers on her table. So I said, 'What's all this stuff?'

And she said, 'Well, it's kinda like flying stuff.'

I said, 'Well I've never seen it here before.'

And she said, 'Well, you know I'm kinda like maybe I'm thinking about flying across the country.'

I said, 'What?! Vicki, you're kidding, right?' She kids around a lot and I thought she was just joking.

She said, 'No, I'm not kidding.'

I said, 'That's impossible!'

She said, 'No, it's not. I think I'm gonna do it.'

And I said, 'Okay, cool.' She told me not to tell anybody."

On the last day of school, my teacher Mrs. Nydes asked everyone in the class to stand up and say what we planned to do for the summer. This kid Jonathan stood up and said, "I'm going to go collect some turtles." Somebody else said they were going to do a lot of swimming.

Mrs. Nydes called my name. I stood up and said, "I don't know if this is going to happen, so don't tell anybody. I'll look like a dork if I don't do it. But what I hope to do is fly a plane across the country."

25

Bob and I are set to take off on our cross-country journey.

3

"She may be the honorary mayor of Oklahoma City, but she still has to clean her room."

At first, my folks were not exactly thrilled at the idea of me flying cross-country. The trip would take almost a week, so I'd have to stay in hotels. We'd have to work out a schedule for them to follow me in commercial airliners so that we could be together at night. And it would be an expensive trip. I think they hoped I was just kidding when I first brought up the idea.

But as the summer went on, I became more and more excited about flying across the United States. One day my dad said to me, "Vicki, is this something you really have your heart set on doing?" I told him how much the trip would mean to me.

"Then let's do it," he said. "We'll find a way to pull it off."

Planning any trip is just as important as flying the plane. From my own experience flying, I figured that September would be the best month of the year to go cross-country. It's not too hot, so you don't hit a lot of turbulence in the air. And it's not too cold, so you don't have to worry about running into snow.

I had ten weeks to get ready. The summer would give me the chance to get in a lot of practice flying. I began taking lessons two, sometimes three times a week.

I ordered maps of the entire United States to plan where I'd stop for fuel and where I'd sleep at night. Pilots don't use regular road maps. They use sectional aeronautical charts, maps that describe every airport in the area, the distances between them, radio frequencies, and other information you need to know if you're flying in that area. For example, four little dots by an airport means you can get fuel there.

Some larger airports charge you anywhere from $5–$25 to land. At smaller airports, it doesn't cost anything and you can just radio in when you're about five miles away.

The maps were each about five feet by two feet and I needed ten of them to cover the entire country. I taped the maps up all over the wall in our downstairs hallway so I could see the whole trip at once.

There are a lot of things to consider in planning out a trip like this. I'd have to make a few stops at major cities where the commercial planes land so my parents could join me along the way. Between the major cities, I wanted to land at small airports where there wouldn't be a lot of traffic. And I didn't want to fly much more than 800 miles in a day.

Before any long trip you have to calculate your fuel requirements. For example, single-engine planes burn about 13 gallons of fuel in an hour of flying. Say the fuel tanks hold 45 gallons and the plane cruises at 150 miles per hour. If you divide 45 by 13, you get 3.46, which is the number of hours you can fly before you have to come down and refuel. To find out the maximum distance you can fly on each leg of the trip, you multiply the 3.46 times the speed of the plane— 150 miles an hour. That equals 519 miles. When you plan the trip, you have to make sure your stops are no more than 500 or so miles apart.

There's a lot of math involved in flying. Fortunately, I like math.

There are several ways to cross the United States. I wanted to fly east to west because it's harder that way. You have to fly mostly against the wind, and the time changes are harder to get used to.

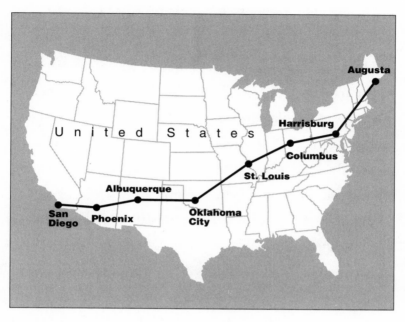

I picked the Augusta to San Diego route because I wanted to fly the longest possible distance—3,000 miles—across the country.

I chose a route that would take me from the northeast tip of the nation—Augusta, Maine—to the southwest tip—San Diego, California. That way, I'd have to fly the longest possible distance—3,000 miles. I wanted to make it tough on myself.

I would stop for fuel, food, and bathroom every three and a half hours, with overnight stops in Columbus, Ohio; Oklahoma City, Oklahoma; and Phoenix, Arizona. I would try to fly eight hours each day. Actually, you're only *allowed* to fly eight hours a day, because flight instructors are only allowed to work eight hours a day. I also made it a goal to complete the trip in three and a half days. That would be a real challenge.

Once again, Bob Baumgartner agreed to accompany me on the trip. I remember my folks felt Bob could have helped me more at the planning stage of the trip, but they came to realize he didn't help much on purpose. Planning is a big part of flying. If he had planned the flight for me, I couldn't honestly say I flew across the country.

The only thing I couldn't plan was the weather. I had to hope for the best.

I learned to fly in a Cessna 150, but I needed a more powerful plane to take me across the country. My parents rented a used Cessna 172 from the Meadville Aero Flight School at Port Meadville Airport. It's faster and heavier (it weighs 1,500 pounds) than the 150, with a 160 horsepower engine that can cruise at 130 miles per hour.

It cost $60 an hour to rent the plane. That's $60 for every hour spent *flying*. You don't pay for the time the plane spends on the ground.

The plane was twenty-five feet long, and it was white with green and mustard colored stripes. It was twenty-eight years old, which is *ancient* for a car, and pretty old for a plane too. It had no autopilot, so the pilot would have to pay attention to the flying constantly.

The Cessna 172 has a higher instrument panel than the

150, which made it a little hard for me to see out the windshield. I put two thick cushions on my seat and that seemed to solve the problem.

There was one small problem with flying in September—that's when school starts. I had just begun sixth grade. I would have to miss some school, and there would be no time to do any homework during the trip.

My new teachers, Mrs. Diane Dowler and Mrs. Marie Rozakis, were terrific about it. We made arrangements for me to stay after school when I got back to make up the work I was going to miss. They even came by my house to tell me not to worry about my schoolwork while I was away. And my mom had been a teacher, so she agreed to give me some tutoring along the way.

Besides, often while waiting to go to the airport or in the hotel room at night, I would have some time to kill. I always made sure to take books along. Science fiction and mystery are my favorites. I really liked the *Star Wars* movies, and that made me want to read stories based on the characters. I would also take along some magazines, like *Sports Illustrated for Kids* and *Disney Adventures*.

I always liked to read. When I was younger my favorite book was *Alice in Wonderland* by Lewis Carroll. I also read a lot of Nancy Drew, and I was into *Goosebumps* and those scary Christopher Pike books a few years ago. Crossword puzzle books are fun too. A lot of girls read *The Babysitters Club* when I was little, but I never liked that stuff.

Grownups are always telling kids that reading will help us get good grades in school, get into college, get a good career, and things like that. But for me, I like to read simply because it's fun. When I lose myself in a good story, I don't have to think about the weather over the Rockies, ice forming on the wings of the plane, or tomorrow's flight plan for a little while.

Anyway the day before the trip, my class threw me a surprise party. The kids made a big banner that read "Good Luck Vicki," and everybody autographed it. Jenny Gifford made little airplanes out of candy. There were cupcakes. Mrs. Dowler and Mrs. Rozakis gave me a silver dollar for good luck.

Meadville, Pennsylvania: With the sendoff that Meadville gave me on September 18, you would think I had invented the zipper or something. The city held a press conference, and all the local politicians came out to the airport to give me flowers and plaques. There were also some reporters and photographers.

Bob Swanson, the guy I had the doughnut wars with in flight school, showed up with his wife. He wished me luck and said, "I have something for you." Then he pulled out a bag of coconut doughnuts and handed it to me.

I had been told in advance that I would be asked to say a few words, so I had prepared a short speech. I thanked everyone and told them I was proud to be Meadville's ambassador. I ended the speech with the words, "Someone once said every accomplishment, great or small, starts with the right decision. That decision is, I'll try. That's what I'm going to do. I'm going to try my best."

My sister was away at school, so she couldn't see me off. I wanted to hug my brother and my parents, but I felt embarrassed doing it in front of all those people.

Bob and I got into the plane. We said our good-byes and took off.

Before heading away from Meadville, I did a "flyby" for the crowd. That's when you dive down and buzz low over the runway. It was pretty cool.

The flight to Augusta was smooth. Along the way we stopped for fuel in Oneonta, New York. My folks took a commercial flight and met me when I landed at Augusta State Airport.

Augusta, Maine: My plan was to get up at 5:00 each morning, get to the airport by 6:00, and be in the air by 7:00. I figured that would be the hardest part of the trip. I'm a bit of a night person, and I usually sleep until 11:00 in the morning—if my mom lets me. But I would never be able to fly 800 miles a day and reach San Diego in four days if I woke up so late.

I was excited thinking about the trip, and I was jumping up and down on the bed in the hotel room long after I should have been asleep. When 5:00 A.M. rolled around, my parents practically had to pour cold water over my face to get me out of bed. I didn't feel all that great, but I figured it was just nerves.

I pulled on my olive brown flight suit, which Bob had ordered from an ad in a magazine. It's not very fashionable, but it has about ten pockets on it, which come in handy for storing stuff. I ate some Froot Loops for breakfast. My dad went out and brought back a bag of peaches for me to snack on in the plane.

Before leaving the hotel, I called to check the weather and file my flight plan with the Federal Aviation Administration—tell them who I am, what my course will be, what time I expect to arrive, and things like that. I would do this every morning of the trip. While I was waiting to go to the airport, I hung out watching Garfield cartoons on TV.

It was a beautiful, clear Maine day, but it was really windy and cold. I hadn't expected any festivities in Augusta, but the news media had picked up on the story and when I got to the plane it was surrounded by reporters, photographers, and well-wishers. Microphones and cameras were shoved in my face and questions were flying at me from every direction. People handed me pieces of paper to sign. It felt very strange signing autographs, like I was a real celebrity.

Peter Thompson, the president of the Augusta Chamber of Commerce, presented me with a bottle of water from the Atlantic Ocean. He asked me to pour it into the Pacific Ocean when I got there. I stored the bottle of water in the pocket behind my seat. Some people gave me keychains and pins. I put the keychains in my pocket and stuck the pins on my flight suit.

I was introduced to a remarkable eighty-year-old lady

Veda Grant came out to see me off.

named Veda Grant. In 1936, she was the first female to fly solo from this airport. Veda only gave up flying a few years ago when her eyesight started to fail her. She told me how proud of me she was and pulled a worn and tattered patch from her pocket that looked like it had seen a lot of flights. It said, "God is my copilot." Veda had tears in her eyes as she handed me the patch. I put it in my pocket and kept it there the entire trip. To this day, I keep it in that pocket every time I fly.

I was shivering and my fingers felt like they were freezing as I talked with the reporters, who never seemed to run out of questions. The wind-chill factor made it feel like the temperature was below zero. Peter Thompson loaned me his coat.

I tried to be polite to everyone, but I had work to do. Before every flight, the pilot does a preflight inspection of the plane. I checked the propeller for nicks, made sure the elevators could move freely, and checked the oil. You do this the same way you do it on a car, with a dipstick and a rag. You also have to check for fuel leaks and hydraulic leaks, and make sure the tires have the correct amount of air in them.

Every so often, a bird will build a nest in a plane's engine, and this can be dangerous if you don't take it out. I've never had that happen to me, but I have had to get rid of spiderwebs in the engine.

I said my good-byes to everybody, and Bob and I climbed into the plane. The newspeople kept asking questions and taking pictures until finally I just had to close the door on them. It was a relief to get into the air. But it was also pretty neat, I had to admit to myself, that so many people would hear about my trip. It was 7:21 A.M. when we took off.

The sky was perfectly clear, and soon I could even see Manhattan, with its twin towers of the World Trade Center, in the distance. Along the way to Harrisburg, Pennsylvania, the trees looked like broccoli.

Harrisburg, Pennsylvania: There are two rolling mountains when you approach the Capitol City airport, and I flew right between them. We arrived in Harrisburg at 12:30, right on time. My godmother Alice and state senator Bob Robbins were there to meet the plane. After a short break, we took off on the next leg of the journey, to Columbus, Ohio.

On the way to Columbus, I began to feel a little hungry and pulled out those peaches my dad had given me in Augusta. I put one in my mouth and it was so hard I couldn't even break the skin with my teeth. My dad, I remembered, is terrible about picking fruit. The peaches wouldn't be ripe until the whole trip was over. I threw them in the back of the plane.

Otherwise, the flight to Columbus was routine. The trip

was going along very smoothly. But that was about to change.

Columbus, Ohio: It was clear and sunny when we touched down at Port Columbus International Airport. I began to feel symptoms of a cold coming on. My nose was stuffed up, so I had to breathe through my mouth. That's not good for your ears, and I'm prone to ear infections.

The fact that Bob was a chain smoker didn't help. He tried to cut down, but three hours is a long time, and he lit up while we were flying. It's a very small cabin in the plane, and the smoke bothered me.

It was not a good time to get sick. We were heading into the tough part of the trip, over the unpredictable weather of the Rockies and the Arizona desert.

My parents took me out for dinner at a restaurant in Columbus. We sat there a long time waiting to be served, and all I wanted to do was go to bed. I tried to hide it from my folks, but they could see I was sniffing almost constantly and they were concerned about my health.

After about an hour of waiting to order, my dad stood up and shouted, "Can we get some service please? We've got a girl here who's flying across the country and she needs some food and rest!"

One of the waitresses rushed over and said, "Hey, you're the little girl I saw on TV!" The management apologized all over the place, and they hopped to it. I guess fame has its rewards.

I was making fun of my dad because of the underripe peaches he'd given me when a guy named Stan came over to our table and asked for my autograph. He was really nice, and when I got to the hotel after dinner, I found he had sent tons of peaches, plums, and bananas to our room. I named him Stan the Fruit Man.

I was still feeling lousy when I went to bed that night. To make matters worse, there was a ringing in my ears. It was the noise of the plane's engine. After flying for so many hours, it was starting to get to me.

I know my dad was up all night listening to my wheezing and worrying about me. I'm sure he was thinking of calling the rest of the trip off, but he knew I'd have none of that. I got up at 5:00 A.M. and headed for the airport. The skies were overcast, cold, and rainy. That's how I felt, too.

My mood improved when we were greeted at the airport by our new friend Stan the Fruit Man. Actually, he's a Sunday school teacher who flies planes as a hobby. Stan brought along one of his students who was interested in flying, a fourteen-year-old girl named Kaylen Conley, and her family. Stan gave me a bouquet of flowers and Kaylen gave me a tiny Bible that fit in the palm of my hand. It came with a little magnifying glass so you could read it.

Stan and the Conleys were all so cheerful, they gave me the boost I needed to get through the day.

St. Louis, Missouri: This was the summer of 1993, when the midwest was hit by devastating floods. From the air, it was an incredible sight. The Mississippi River had over-flowed its banks, and muddy water was all over the place. I saw buildings of which only the roof was above water. There were telephone poles sticking up out of the water.

My class had been studying the Great Plains. I pulled out my camera and took pictures of it all so I could show them to everybody when I got home. I held the yoke with my right hand and the camera with my left.

The skies had cleared, and the sun was so bright we put the visors down so we could see. Bob put his sunglasses on. I didn't, because I look dorky in sunglasses.

We were due for a noon fuel stop at Spirit of St. Louis Field, but it was almost completely under water. I had known that might happen, and had a backup airport in case I would need it—Lambert Field. There was no problem landing there. I felt myself becoming sicker, but I pressed on to Oklahoma City.

Vicki's Dad Jim

"We were still having a hard time believing this was for real. I picked up a St. Louis paper at the airport newsstand

I wasn't old enough to vote, but I was old enough to be the honorary mayor of Oklahoma City.

and there was an article about Vicki in there. Then I picked up a Columbus paper and there was another story about Vicki. And then I picked up The New York Times *and her picture was staring back at me. The story was sweeping the country before our eyes."*

Oklahoma City, Oklahoma: We landed at Wiley Post Airport around 5:00 P.M. Wiley Post made the first solo flight around the world in 1933. Two years later he was killed in a crash in Alaska. Will Rogers was a passenger on the plane.

My flight had somehow become a national story, and the crowd of press people and dignitaries was growing with every stop I made.

I was welcomed to Oklahoma City by the 99ers Club, a group of female flyers that was formed by Amelia Earhart. They presented me with "Amelia Bear-heart," a stuffed bear wearing flight goggles and boots. My dad had been buying stuffed animals for me along the way too, and my collection was getting enormous.

I was named honorary mayor of Oklahoma City. My dad made the local news when somebody asked him how he felt and he replied, "She may be the honorary mayor of Oklahoma City, but she still has to clean her room when she gets home."

I was starting to settle into a routine for the trip. Every night, after all the excitement of the day, I would finally get to bed around 10:00 P.M. My poor dad usually got up at 2:00 A.M. so he could get food and deal with all the requests for interviews that were coming in.

We tried not to turn anybody down. One morning I got up at 4:00 to do a telephone interview with a radio station in Bogata, Columbia. I must have been out of my mind. A lot of stations wanted to have me on their morning talk shows. I was getting pretty good at giving interviews, and I was able to do a radio show over the phone at the same time

I was getting dressed and eating breakfast. Then I'd call for the weather and head off for the next day of flying.

I had a slice of pizza that night, but I was really sick and didn't even bother trying to hide it from my folks anymore. They called my doctor back home and got some nasal spray and antibiotics.

The trip was half over. I was determined to finish it, no matter how sick I became. I didn't realize it at the time, but the worst was yet to come.

Touching down in San Diego.

4

"They ground pilots for a
lot less than you have."

I had flown over the Appalachian Mountains when I went to my sister's graduation, but they were nothing compared to the Rockies. Passing over them was *incredible*. There were hundreds of brown and red peaks, some of them really sharp and tipped with snow.

Every so often a thin road would snake through the mountains, and then there would be two or three houses in the middle of nowhere. I couldn't imagine who would want to live out there. I didn't want to imagine a plane ever going down out there.

Unfortunately, I was too busy flying the plane to enjoy

the view. The weather was getting rough. The headwind, the wind coming toward the plane, was getting close to forty knots. The plane was starting to bounce around. My stomach felt queasy. I took out an airsickness bag and put it on my lap in case I needed to throw up.

Because of the headwind, it was taking us longer to plow through the air than I had calculated. The engine had to work harder. I decided to make an unscheduled fuel stop in Tucumcari, New Mexico, which is 175 miles east of Albuquerque. Then we set off again.

Finally, the weather broke and Albuquerque's Double Eagle II Airport came into view. I was exhausted. My brain was tired from such intense concentration. We were an hour late, and we still had to get to Phoenix by the end of the day. I tried to have a bite to eat, but I couldn't keep anything down. There was nothing to do but fill 'er up and keep flying.

At the height of the Rockies, I was flying at 12,000 feet when the plane hit *severe* turbulence. The wind was throwing us up and down 200 feet in a single second. It felt like a roller coaster, except that we didn't know when it would be over.

Bob took over the radio so I could concentrate on controlling the plane. There was no way I was going to ask him to take over the controls. It would nullify all I had accomplished. There wasn't anything Bob could do anyway. The situation was out of our control.

I was trying to forget that I was sick, but it wasn't working. I couldn't hold back anymore and vomited, clutching the yoke in one hand and the barf-bag in the other. It was pretty disgusting.

We couldn't fly higher, because the air gets very thin up high and we would need oxygen. We couldn't fly lower, or we'd hit the mountains. We just had to tough it out.

My stomach was not cooperating. I threw up again. My insides felt empty.

Phoenix, Arizona: I had hoped that once we got past the Rocky Mountains the air would settle down, but it didn't. When the sun's rays hit the Arizona desert, they bounced up, changed the air temperature and formed air pockets. So we had another bumpy flight on our hands. As an added attraction, it was brutally hot in the plane and there was no air conditioning.

I had been keeping an eye on the fuel and once again decided to make an unscheduled stop. There aren't a lot of airports across the desert, so it was either stop at St. John's, Arizona, which is midway between Albuquerque and Phoenix, or risk running out of fuel.

Another problem was that I was becoming dehydrated. That was my own fault. I didn't want to have to use my portable toilet, so I was being careful not to drink too much during the trip. If my parents had been with me, I'm sure they would have told me to keep drinking fluids. But they weren't. In any case, I filled my third barf-bag and I was feeling worse than I had ever felt in my life.

I still had to land the plane, which took all my concentration. I know I had tears in my eyes, but I turned my face toward the window so Bob wouldn't see.

"Do you want me to take over?" Bob asked as we got close to Phoenix.

"No," I replied. "I'll land it."

Realizing that I wasn't going to be talked into giving up the controls, Bob must have decided I would need a pep talk.

"You've come this far," he told me. "You have to do this. If you bounce it, that's okay. Just put it down."

I was really grateful to have Bob with me. I had logged about sixty hours of flying by then, but most of it had been close to home. Bob's advice and his experience in long distance flying helped me through some really tough times on this trip.

It wasn't my prettiest landing at Sky Harbor Airport in Phoenix, but I managed to bring it down. It was 5:45 P.M. We were a couple of hours late. I knew everybody on the ground was really worried, especially my parents.

I had known all along that the mountains and desert would be difficult to fly over, but they had been so much worse than I expected.

I had battled heat, turbulence, airsickness, and a cold all at the same time. I just hoped the toughest part of the trip was over.

I stepped out of the plane carefully, waving and smiling like it had all been a stroll in the park. For once, I walked right past the reporters and microphones that were shoved in my face. Somebody told the press that I needed five minutes before I could answer their questions and pose for pictures.

I found my mom in the crowd and she led me to a bathroom. There was no place to lie down, but that was okay. I needed a sink to lean over anyway.

Vicki's Dad Jim

"Our friend Linda was traveling with us. She came out of the bathroom and said to me, 'Jim, I don't think she's going to be able to come out.' I figured it was all over. She had come close, but the trip was finished. I went inside and saw Vicki dry heaving into a sink. She looked up at me with tears streaming down her face and said, 'Dad, if I could just have two more minutes and a little bit of water I can go out there.'"

I felt pretty crummy, but I came out and pretended to be fine, answering all the reporters' questions and posing for the cameras for forty-five minutes.

I didn't want to tell them how tough it had been. My feeling is that a real pilot—of any age—doesn't complain about flying. I knew what I was getting into when I decided to learn how to fly. I had known that sometimes it would be difficult.

The only hint I gave of how much trouble I'd had was when I told the reporters, "I knew this wasn't going to be easy, and it wasn't."

I was asked to sign a logbook of celebrities who had been to the airport. As I was about to write my name, I glanced up and saw the signature above mine: Charles Barkley.

My parents suggested we wait a few days so I could recuperate before continuing on to San Diego. I said no way. When I start something, I want to finish it. My plan was to fly across the country in three and a half days. In my mind, if I took a break, I would not have achieved my goal. And I was so close to achieving it.

I'd been flying ten hours a day for three days (in spite of the 8 hour flight rule), and I was only getting five hours of sleep a night. The changes as we moved across time zones were messing me up too. After landing in Phoenix, I was totally drained and all I wanted to do was get to bed. But my folks saw what kind of shape I was in, and they insisted on taking me to a doctor that night.

The doctor made us spend half an hour filling out forms, and then he took one look at me and said he wanted me to go to an emergency room at a hospital.

"They ground pilots for a lot less than you have," he said sternly.

I knew that if I went to an emergency room, my trip would be over. They would keep me in the hospital overnight. The doctors there would insist that I not fly, because if anything happened to me, people would say it was *their* fault.

My folks told me I had accomplished a lot flying from Maine to Phoenix, and assured me that it was okay if I called the rest of the trip off.

I said no way. I'd worked so hard to get this far, and I wasn't going to give up now. Not with one three-hour flight to San Diego standing between me and my goal.

The doctor said he was going to give me a shot to settle my stomach. I started rolling up a sleeve and he said, "Pull down your pants."

"Why should I pull down my pants?" I asked.

"Because I'm giving you a shot in your behind."

"My behind feels fine," I told him. "It's my stomach that's bothering me."

But I didn't argue very long. He did what he had to do. We went back to the hotel and I was able to hold down some Jell-O and some soup. I was feeling a little better. I didn't have to get up early, so I was able to get my first good night's sleep in a week.

San Diego, California: We took off at 11:00 A.M. for the final leg of the journey. The air was clear and there was hardly any wind. What a relief it was after what I'd been through the day before! I was able to enjoy the scenery. At one point I saw a hawk chasing a rabbit across the desert, trying to catch it with its claws.

San Diego is right next to the Mexican border, and it was exciting to see another country from the cockpit of the plane.

There were no problems at all on this final leg of the flight. I banked the Cessna over the mountains and landed smoothly at Montgomery Field.

It was over. My goal had been to fly from one tip of the nation to the other in three and a half days, and I had accomplished it. I felt great.

The crowds that greeted me at the airports in Oklahoma

Not only did I receive gifts along the way, I also gave away memorabilia from Meadville.

City and Phoenix were big, but in San Diego it was a *crush* of people. At first I thought the President was in town or something.

I was presented with the key to the city, plaques, flowers, and gifts. During the trip I had started collecting keychains wherever I landed. By the end, I had twenty-five. I had also been accumulating pins, and my dad said I looked like a Guatemalan general. I was lucky I didn't have to go through metal detectors at the airports.

A ninety-year-old former pilot named Bobbie Trout introduced herself to me. She had competed against Amelia Earhart in flying contests back in the 1930s. Shamu (actually a guy in an enormous whale suit) shook my hand and invited me to Sea World. I was introduced to a nine-year-old girl who told me she was going to be a pilot too.

My folks checked us into the hotel and so many flowers had been sent to the room that it looked like somebody had died.

Ever since the trip began, people had been giving me flowers, balloons, and other gifts. I didn't know what to do with them all, and I got the idea that maybe we could send them to children's hospitals to help some kids get better who are having a hard time. That's one of the nicest things about this sudden fame, I realized; I could use it to do good things.

I curled up on the bed with my mom and watched TV. My cross-country flight was all over the news. It was weird flipping from one channel to the next and seeing my face on every one.

"Just think," one newscaster said, "in five years she can get her driver's license."

Vicki's Mother Corinne

"Vicki doesn't often say how she feels inside. But that night when we went to bed the lights were out, it was very quiet, and

It was such a relief to see my mom and dad in San Diego. But I think they were more nervous than I was!

she had all her stuffed animals around her. I was next to her on the bed and we were just enjoying this lovely moment in our lives. She said to me, 'You know Mom, I want to do something with children's hospitals.' I was so taken aback. We had never discussed anything like that before. When we left the hotel, we had all the flowers in the room sent to a children's hospital."

When I first decided to fly cross-country, I wasn't aware of any aviation records, and I hadn't set out to break any. The F.A.A. doesn't keep records for pilots younger than sixteen. Neither does *The Guinness Book of World Records*. They're probably afraid kids might steal planes and try to fly them.

But somebody did some research and discovered that I had set three aviation records. I was the youngest female pilot to fly across the United States (a nine-year-old boy named Tony Aliengena flew across the country in 1988) and the youngest pilot to fly coast to coast from east to west, and I had flown the farthest distance of any child. I have to admit that setting the records made me feel even better about what I had accomplished.

The excitement of the trip was over, and I had the chance to relax and do some sightseeing with my parents. We visited Sea World and Disneyland. The press continued to follow me, and there was a funny picture of me in one newspaper piloting Dumbo, the Flying Elephant.

There was one more thing I had to do in California. During the entire trip, I had saved the bottle of water from the Atlantic Ocean that had been given to me back in Maine. My folks and I took a walk to the beach and poured the water into the Pacific Ocean. I felt it symbolized the unity of our country.

While I was at it, I refilled the bottle with Pacific Ocean water. Someday, I thought, I'll pour it into the Atlantic Ocean and complete the circle.

———

Before we headed back to Meadville, I received an invitation to visit NASA's Johnson Space Center in Houston, Texas. For an aspiring astronaut, this was a dream come true.

Bob flew the Cessna to Shreveport, Louisiana by himself while I took a commercial airliner there with my parents. It was nice having somebody *else* fly the plane for a change. But I wanted to fly to NASA myself, so I piloted the plane from Shreveport to Houston. I was given permission to land at Ellington Field there—the same runway the astronauts use to

After the trip, NASA invited me to visit. They have all kinds of virtual reality simulations of space flight.

land their planes when they come back from Cape Canaveral.

At NASA I met Stephanie Wells, who trains the astronauts. She let me try on an astronaut's parachute and a helmet, which was really heavy.

Astronaut Tammy Jernigan, who has been on a couple of Space Shuttle missions, gave me, Bob, and my parents a great tour. The best part was when she gave me the opportunity to land the space shuttle. Not the real shuttle, of course. It was a simulation, sort of like a video game.

Tammy told me it was really difficult to land successfully, and most of the *astronauts* couldn't even do it the first few

In the cockpit of a T-38 astronaut trainer, with Stephanie Wells standing by.

times. Bob tried the simulator first, and he crashed chin first into the runway. That was enough for him. He didn't want to try again.

There were a bunch of reporters around, and Tammy whispered that maybe I shouldn't try to land the shuttle with that kind of pressure. But after what I'd been through over the last week, playing a video game was no pressure at all. I told her I wanted to try.

My dad and I made a little bet. We agreed that if I could land the space shuttle safely, he would get me a pet ferret. I have a cat named Lucy and a dog named Cricket at home. But I really wanted a ferret.

I almost landed the shuttle cleanly on my first shot. I was just a little bit off and I didn't totally crash. I asked if I could try again, and Tammy said sure. This time I *greased* it. That's pilot talk for a perfect landing. Everybody was cheering.

I reminded my dad that we'd have to go to a pet store as soon as we got home.

I flew the plane back home, and there were about 200 people at the Port Meadville Airport waiting for me. They treated me like a celebrity, with a reception, gifts, plaques, trophies, and certificates. I even received a letter from the president!

I thanked everybody for their support and for coming out

to greet me. One of the local banks sponsored a big reception for everyone. They had fancy food and even a small orchestra. A Meadville artist named "T-shirt Larry" painted a giant "Welcome Home" banner showing me in the plane. They hung it on the downtown mall. Then I went to the movies with my friends. We saw this police movie called *Undercover Blues*. It was great just to do something *normal* for a change.

As promised, my folks took me to a pet store to get the ferret I won by landing the space shuttle. But when we got there, they convinced me that ferrets are dirty and smelly, and you have to clean out their cage all the time. Besides, neighbors of ours had a ferret and it got lost in their house. To this day, they *still* haven't found it. My folks talked me into getting a kitten instead. I picked out a beautiful Siamese and we named her Monique.

What I really want *now* is a dachsund.

5

"How does it feel to be on a big show like mine?"

Before I took off from Augusta on September 20, hardly anybody outside of Meadville knew my name. I wasn't even anything special in *Meadville*! Four days later, most of America had heard about me.

I hadn't won an Olympic medal, saved somebody's life, or killed anyone—the usual ways people become famous quickly. Something about my flight must have touched a nerve. I guess the newspapers are filled with so much bad news day after day that people saw the story of the girl flying across the country as very different and uplifting.

Vicki's Mother Corinne

"Vicki was always a very quiet person. The first time a reporter asked her questions, she kept looking at me and Jim to answer. We knew she could answer the questions better than we could, so we just backed out of the picture. From that time on, she handled all the interviews herself."

I never set out to be famous. It wasn't important to me, and it isn't important to me now. I don't believe people should do something to try and become famous. You should want to do something because it's a challenge, because you want to learn something, or because something inside you tells you you ought to do it. My mission was always to set a challenge for myself and achieve it. That's it.

I must admit, though, it's been kind of fun. If you ever get the chance to become famous, jump on it.

After my third flying lesson, an article about me appeared in the *Meadville Tribune*. It was really exciting to see my name and picture in the paper. They didn't make a big deal about it at school, and I didn't brag about it.

The weekend before the trip, one of the producers of *The Today Show* happened to stop into his office. He saw a short item come over the Associated Press newswire about my upcoming flight across the country. It included the quote:

After I was on The Today Show, *all the other talk shows invited me to be a guest. That's me and my parents with Bryant Gumbel and Katie Couric.*

"Every accomplishment, great or small, starts with the right decision. That decision is, I'll try."

He must have liked the sound of that, because he arranged to have a truck and satellite dish at the airport in Augusta so I could talk live with Bryant Gumbel before I took off.

Other news organizations must have read the same item. When I got to Augusta, there were messages waiting at the hotel from *Inside Edition,* CBS Radio, *The Home Show,* and many others. My dad handled all the calls.

After I appeared on *The Today Show,* everything snow-balled. At every hotel I stopped at, the phone in the room rang constantly. Finally we had to stop taking calls. I would go to sleep and wake up to find thirty or forty messages.

Throughout the trip, dozens of local news shows across the country covered my takeoffs and landings. I have stacks of newspaper articles. I was interviewed by *Time* and *Newsweek*.

With Conan O'Brien.

I spoke with Bryant Gumbel of *The Today Show* again after I reached San Diego. I appeared on *Maury Povich, Late Night with Conan O'Brien* (he was *really* tall!), *Live with Regis &*

Kathie Lee, The John and Leeza Show, and *The Chevy Chase Show.* They wanted me on David Letterman's show, but only if I didn't appear on other talk shows. My dad didn't think that was fair, so we turned them down.

When I sat in the chair next to Chevy Chase, the first question he asked was, "So how does it feel to be on a big show like mine?" I guess he didn't know he was going to be off the air a few months later.

I gave Chevy a souvenir pen from Meadville. He presented me with a bunch of stuff his little daughter had suggested—an airsickness bag, a gallon of milk, and a turkey. It was pretty funny.

People always ask me if I got nervous on these TV shows, knowing that millions of people were watching me. I don't know why, but it never bothered me. My mom used to coach the local high school speech team and my sister is an actress, so I knew what it was like to be in front of an audience.

Even the first time, when I was on *The Today Show* with Bryant Gumbel, it just felt really fun and exciting to me. I never thought, "Oh wow! I can't believe I'm sitting across from Bryant Gumbel!" It was nice to meet these celebrities, but they're just regular people.

I became so comfortable on TV that I made a secret signal

with my grandmother. When I rubbed my chin, that was my way of saying hello to her.

In case you're wondering, TV talk shows pay their guests anywhere from $50 to $400 (*The Tonight Show*) or even $600 (*Live with Regis & Kathie Lee*). We used most of this money to pay for the fuel, renting the plane, and other expenses. I did treat myself to a few things, though. I bought a remote control car at F.A.O. Schwartz, the famous toy store in New York City. Later, when I went to London I bought a Game Boy, which helped pass the time on the long flight home. I also got a Looney Toons blue jean jacket.

The more I appeared on TV, the more people called with invitations to do other appearances. I was flown to England to appear on a show called *Record Breakers*. I threw out the first ball at a Cleveland Indians game. I was invited to spend a week at Space Camp in Huntsville, Alabama. I gave talks before the Pennsylvania State Senate, TRW's National Take Your Daughter to Work Day, the Milk International Children's Festival, and the Women's Sports Foundation at Temple University.

They even made jokes about me on *Saturday Night Live, David Letterman,* and *The Tonight Show.* I didn't hear any of them, but my aunt told me Jay Leno cracked that I was so young, we had to stop the plane every few hours so my

One day Jay Leno told a joke in his monologue about me. Later, he invited me on the show as a guest.

diaper could be changed. It was pretty funny, and later Jay Leno actually invited me on *The Tonight Show*. He was really nice. He looked a little different in person than he does on TV. I can't explain how, but he just did.

Before you go on the air on these shows, you go in a room where you can relax, have a snack, and watch the show as it's being taped. They call it the "green room," but I don't know why because none of them were green. Of all the shows I appeared on, *The Tonight Show* had the best food. They had these strawberries with chocolate and vanilla on them. They were great and I ate a ton of them. *The Chevy Chase Show* had really great food too.

Sometimes when I appeared on these shows, they would take me in a room and put makeup on my face. They'd brush on some powdery stuff so the lights wouldn't reflect off me, and maybe some blush. I don't wear makeup in real life.

My dad's always trying to get me to come into the living room and watch tapes of my TV appearances, but I don't want to. I look a little nerdy on TV. Besides, I was *there*, so why would I want to see it again?

Vicki's Dad Jim

"Just to show you how the media works, this one TV show spent a tremendous amount of time shooting Vicki for a big segment they wanted to do on her. But days and weeks went by and they hadn't run it. I called the producer up and he told me the O.J. Simpson murder case had knocked everything else out of the news. 'Jim,' he said, 'I'll tell you what it would take right now for that story to be aired. If Vicki were to kill you and your wife, I guarantee you that segment will be on tomorrow night.'"

Answering the same questions over and over again got to be a drag at times. "How did you start to fly? What got you interested? When did you think of flying across the country?" It got so I could answer them in my sleep. But I always answered all the questions people asked me, and I posed for as many pictures as they wanted.

The reporters would usually ask something like, "How do you feel?" I got into the habit of responding, "Uh . . . pretty good," and then I'd let out a little laugh. Later I found out

I didn't set out to be famous, but the press picked up the story and the reporters swarmed all over me. One lady followed me into a bathroom to ask questions.

that some reporters started to imitate me, walking around saying "Uh . . . pretty good . . . heh heh." They even competed to see which one could "do me" the best.

The one question I didn't particularly like (but was asked all the time) was, "Do you have a boyfriend?" I *didn't*, and I *don't*, and even if I *did* I wouldn't want to have people hear about it on TV or in the papers.

One magazine brought a trampoline to a photo shoot and had me jumping up and down so they could get a shot of me flying through the air. In St. Louis, a news reporter followed me into the bathroom to ask questions. She ended up writing a story that was totally wrong.

If you ever find yourself suddenly famous, here's some advice in dealing with the press:

- Try to be yourself. Talk like you're talking to one of your friends.
- Don't try to please somebody by saying something that isn't true.
- Be polite and answer their questions. But always remember that the most important thing is what you came there to do. At some point you have to close the door and tell them you have to go.

Vice President Al Gore showed my folks and me this photo of the Earth, which covers an entire wall of his office.

6

"I might do something with the Atlantic. Like fly over it."

With all the training, flying, and appearances, I had missed fifty days of the sixth grade. I didn't feel very good about that. As it turned out, there hadn't been any time for my mom to tutor me during the trip. But afterwards, while we were taking commercial flights to some of the talk shows, she would give me spelling tests and things like that.

I take my schoolwork very seriously and work very hard to get good grades. It would take a lot of hours after school to make up the work I'd missed.

I wasn't sure how I would be treated when I got back. It crossed my mind that some of the kids might feel jealous or

5

6

7

8

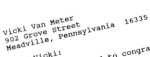

WASHING...

September 30, 1993

Vicki Van Meter
902 Grove Street
Meadville, Pennsylvania   16335

Dear Vicki:

I am delighted to congratulate you on your record-setting flight.

I followed your journey closely and cheered with millions of other Americans as you set three aviation records: the youngest female pilot to fly coast-to-coast across the United States, the youngest pilot to cross the United States from east to west, and the youngest pilot to set a distance record of 2900 miles.

As the city of Meadville welcomes you back and declares this day Vicki Van Meter Day, it gives me great pleasure to commend you on your notable achievement. You are an inspiration to your fellow young Americans, and I know you will meet future challenges just as you have met this one -- courageously and successfully.

Hillary and I send you our best wishes.

Sincerely,

Bill Clinton

9

10

11

12

13

14

1. One of my early flights, at about six months.

2. With Cricket, my miniature German schnauzer.

3. I flew to North Carolina to see my sister Elizabeth (with sunglasses) graduate from high school. Next to me is Rebecca Mesley, my first long-distance passenger.

4. Me and my mom getting a limo ride to ESPN's Arete Awards in Chicago.

5. Meet the press. Bob and I telling the people of Meadville what it was like to fly coast to coast.

6. Me and my sister Elizabeth aboard the aircraft carrier the Dwight D. Eisenhower. We eve got to stay overnight.

7. Being "wired up" to go on a TV show. The wires for the mike had to go under my uniforr

8. Taking off on my transatlantic flight. Destination: Glasgow!

9. I didn't get to meet the president in Washington, but he did send me this letter.

10. When I crossed the country, I brought along small gifts from Meadville to give to digni taries in other towns.

11. Greetings from the mayor of Fismes, France. The French really like kissing!

12. Here I am at the Fitness Warm-Up on National Girls and Women in Sports Day, 1994. Nex to me is a girl who is a professional hockey goalie, next to her is Julie Kron, the jockey.

13. Dad, my brother Daniel, and I were thrilled to meet boxer Evander Holyfield.

14. This is a space shuttle simulator. I wiped out on the first landing, but on my second try greased it!

15. On the way to Greenland. Ice, it turned out, came very close to dragging the plane right into the Atlantic.

act resentful toward me. But as I walked up the steps lead-
ing to school, I realized that wouldn't be a problem. There
was a banner hanging on the railing:

> She flew the country,
> shore to shore.
> East End's Vicki,
> we adore.
> Not in a balloon,
> but in a Cessna plane.
> Vicki Van Meter,
> flew to fame.

I never expected such a big welcome home. There was an
all-school assembly in the cafeteria, where the band played,
the chorus sang, and each class had a student representative
ask me questions about the trip across the country. My class
gave me a necklace with a silver airplane on it, and an avia-
tor bear. My teachers gave me a book on Amelia Earhart,
and the faculty and staff presented me with a book called
Man in Space. Inside was this quote by Louis D. Brandeis:
"Most of the things worth doing in the world had been de-
clared impossible before they were done." The book was in-
scribed, "Vicki, conquer the impossible."

After school that day I invited a couple of kids over, and

I invited a couple of kids over, and the next thing I knew, the whole class was in our backyard!

word somehow got around that there was a party at Vicki's house. I didn't want to tell anybody they couldn't come, and the next thing I knew there were fifty kids in the backyard. I didn't know what to do. My mom was out and my dad was at work. I called him up and told him about the situation.

"Dad, am I in trouble?" I asked.

"Don't be ridiculous," he replied, "Do you want me to bring a couple of pizzas on my way home?"

It was a great party.

The teachers and almost all the kids were wonderful to me when I got back. Mrs. Dowler told me she felt guilty keeping me after school, because I probably learned more in my travels than I would have learned if I spent those fifty days in the classroom.

I wanted to do something nice for everybody, and I got the chance. When I was on *The John and Leeza Show*, somebody asked me what I would wish for if I could have one wish. I said I would like to visit Washington with my classmates and meet the President.

The producers of the show made the arrangements. Some banks in Meadville donated $4,000 and the sixth grade raffled off a bunch of stuff to raise $3,000 more. In November, forty-two kids and nine parents and teachers got on a bus and headed for Washington.

It was a great trip. We visited the Capitol Building, the Vietnam Memorial, and the Lincoln Memorial. Some of the kids wanted to climb up on Abraham Lincoln's lap, but we weren't allowed. Our hotel pool was shaped like a banana.

I have a poster of John F. Kennedy in my room at home, and it was a big thrill to visit Arlington National Cemetery where he is buried. It happened that we arrived on the thirtieth anniversary of his assassination, and Ethel Kennedy and several other members of the Kennedy family were there to honor him. The Secret Service asked us to move so we could give the Kennedys their privacy.

President Clinton was out of town while we were in

Here I am telling Al Gore how to run the country.

Washington, but we got a tour of the White House and I got to meet Vice President Al Gore, who was really tall, and funny too. He showed me a purple Muppet that looks like him. He also has this huge painting of the Earth that fills an entire wall of his office. He's big on environmental issues, and so am I.

Later that day we met Senator John Glenn, who was the first American astronaut to orbit the Earth back in 1962. He was also a pilot during World War II and the Korean War. He told me about the small plane he used to fly when he was just a little older than me.

I asked Senator Glenn about his flight into space. He told me there were some problems with his capsule when he was coming down for re-entry to the Earth's atmosphere. I asked him if he was scared when it was happening, and he replied, "Who wouldn't be?"

Hearing him talk about his experiences was a big thrill for me. Books can only say so much.

Meeting Senator John Glenn was a big thrill.

One day in February, I came into my classroom and a bunch of kids were gathered around my desk. This boy named Eli Provost had taken it upon himself to scan all the papers and clip out articles about me. Eli and the rest of the class were reading a new clipping. It was about that nine-year-old girl I had met in San Diego. She wasn't kidding when she told me she wanted to become a pilot—the clipping said she'd flown a plane across the country.

One of my records had been broken.

The kids in school thought I was going to be upset about it, but I really didn't care. My goal had never been to set any record. I just wanted to fly across the country. If I inspired that girl or anybody else to take up a challenge and achieve it, that made me happy.

In everyday life, people don't always ask each other what they're going to do next. But when you do something that makes the news, I discovered, suddenly *everybody* wants to know. "What are you going to do next? What are you going to do next?" It's as if what you just did doesn't matter anymore.

What I really wanted to do next was hang out at home, shoot baskets with my brother Daniel, watch TV (*Wings* is my favorite show), go to the movies, and do other ordinary kid stuff. I didn't want to disappoint anybody with boring stuff like that, so I just said I didn't know what I wanted to do next.

As 1994 wore on, I began to feel like I wanted to tackle another challenge. I started to think seriously about what it would be. After flying cross-country, there was an obvious challenge waiting for me.

The next time somebody asked what I would do next, I said, "I might do something with the Atlantic Ocean. Like fly over it."

A few last-minute words of advice from my mom before taking off to cross the Atlantic.

7

"Every time she went up I was afraid I'd never see her again."

Naturally, it's harder to fly across an ocean than it is to fly across a country. For one thing, there's not much to look at when you're going over 2,200 miles of water. No landmarks guide your way.

More importantly, ocean crossings are *dangerous*.

When you fly over land, there are airports all over the place. If you can't find an airport and you have to make an emergency landing, you can always bring the plane down on a highway or field or something. Ambulances will be there in seconds. If you have a serious problem in the middle of the ocean, there's not a lot of help around.

Communications are also more difficult over the ocean. There's no radar tracking, so you have to radio in your position to oceanic control, the air traffic control facility that's responsible for separating transatlantic air traffic so that planes don't run into each other.

The English language is used by air traffic controllers around the world, but they all have different accents that are sometimes hard to understand.

I've started taking foreign languages in school, but when I was preparing for the trip I didn't know much beyond *bonjour* and *sayonara*. That also made it harder to read overseas charts and maps. I memorized a few foreign phrases for when I met people on the ground, and I printed these phrases on note cards in case I forgot them.

I began to plan the trip. There are two basic ways to cross the Atlantic: north and south. If you go south the weather is more comfortably warm. But there are much longer distances to cover between landing stops. If you go north, you can "island hop" across the ocean—from the United States, to Canada, to Greenland, to Iceland, and finally to Europe.

I decided to go north. For one thing, I would have needed a much larger single engine plane or a twin engine plane to make it all the way across in one flight. I'd never flown a twin-engine, and it would take months to learn. I also thought it would be more interesting and challenging to

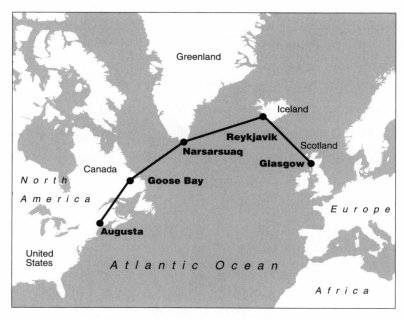

It's easier to fly straight across the ocean, but I decided to island hop.

island hop across the ocean.

I planned a route that would take me from Augusta, Maine, to Goose Bay, Canada, to Narsarsuak, Greenland, to Reykjavik, Iceland, and finish the Atlantic crossing in Glasgow, Scotland.

Other Atlantic Crossings

Many people think Charles Lindbergh was the first person to fly a plane across the Atlantic Ocean. Actually, lots of people made the trip before he did. But Lindbergh was the first to do it solo.

The first successful flight across the Atlantic took place in 1919, when six men flew from Newfoundland to Portugal in a four-engine U.S. Navy "flying boat." Lindbergh made his trip in 1927, and a year later Amelia Earhart became the first woman passenger to fly across. In 1932, on the fifth anniversary of Lindbergh's flight, she became the first woman to fly solo across the Atlantic.

The first passenger flight across the Atlantic was in 1939, the first helicopter in 1952, and the first balloon in 1978.

Many men and women were killed trying to set these records. The year after Charles Lindbergh's flight, fourteen people died trying to duplicate his feat, including three women.

I had turned twelve, which left me four years short of being allowed to fly solo. I needed an instructor to accompany me.

Bob Baumgartner was a good instructor, but he told my parents he wouldn't attempt to fly the Atlantic in a single-engine plane, with or without me. He said it was too dangerous. I know my parents were nervous too, but they gave me their go-ahead to make the trip.

We talked with a number of people we'd met, and found an instructor through an unexpected source—Stan the Fruit Man, the guy who had been so nice to me on the cross-country trip. Stan suggested a pilot he knew in Columbus, Ohio, named Curt Arnspiger.

We called Curt, and a week later he came to Meadville to meet us and talk about the trip. I felt comfortable with Curt right away. He had a real easygoing manner. His daughter, Kayleigh, is a few years younger than me. And he was a non-smoker!

Curt is thirty-eight years old and has been flying since he was in his early twenties. He wanted to be an Air Force pilot when he was younger, but they wouldn't take him because he doesn't have perfect vision. Actually, flying is only Curt's hobby. He makes his living by buying old apartment houses, fixing them up, and selling them, and he's very successful at it.

Curt had experience flying over the ocean, which was important. As a sideline, he delivers airplanes to people in eastern Europe, especially people in oppressed countries like Croatia who may want to leave in a hurry. He had already flown and delivered eight single-engine planes across the Atlantic.

That's how we got the plane for this trip. The Cessna 172 I had flown across the country wasn't powerful enough to handle the weather and flying conditions I'd encounter over the Atlantic. Curt had recently purchased a Cessna 210, which is a bigger, stronger plane. He knew of a possible buyer in Germany. I would be able to train in the plane and fly it across the Atlantic, and Curt could continue on to deliver it to its new owner. It was perfect.

The Cessna 210's engine is 300 horsepower, and the plane can cruise at 170 miles per hour. It's harder to fly than the Cessna 172. The power of the propeller pulls the plane to the left when you take off and land, so you have to compensate for that. It requires more strength. I'm pretty strong, but then again, at the time I weighed less than one hundred pounds. It's a 3,800 pound plane.

Curt said switching from the Cessna 172 to the Cessna 210 is like going from a Chevy Cavalier to a pickup truck without power steering. I've never driven a car, but I got the idea.

The fuel tanks hold ninety-eight gallons. That wouldn't be enough. The airport in Greenland is frequently fogged in and if I couldn't land there I would have to fly 1,500 miles straight from Canada to Iceland.

We arranged to have four of the plane's six seats removed and a hundred gallon fuel tank installed in their place. With the extra fuel, we would be able to make it all the way across to Iceland if we had to.

There's an old wise saying among pilots: Nothing is more useless than fuel back in the fuel truck.

We were thinking about putting a little curtain up in case

The extra fuel tank took up most of the room in the plane.

one of us had to go to the bathroom and wanted privacy, but decided not to. It was a long trip, but the stops would not be too far apart.

I had braces on my teeth back then, and every month the orthodontist would let me pick out two colored rubber bands for the brackets. The Cessna was (and still is) white with red and blue stripes, so that month I picked red and blue rubber bands for my braces.

Written on the side of the plane was N127S, but my dad suggested I give it a name. The whole family sat around dreaming up goofy names, and the best ones I was able to come up with were Murphy and SOS Sassy.

My instructor Curt Arnspiger with my parents.

One day I was reading a book and noticed the bookmark had a bunch of animals on it. At the bottom was the word *harmony*. That sounded like a pretty good name to me. Harmony has a lot of positive meanings. Harmony with music. Harmony with nature. Harmony between nations. I decided to go with it. My dad ordered a gold "Harmony" decal from a company in Denver and we put it on the plane.

From the Transatlantic Flight
Requirements Pamphlet

"Flights by light aircraft across the North Atlantic have increased dramatically in the past few years. Unfortunately,

there has also been a corresponding increase in the number of general aviation search and rescue incidents and aircraft lost.

"Because of the harsh climate, lack of ground-based radio and navigation aids, as well as the immense distances involved, a transatlantic flight is a serious undertaking.

"As you proceed northeast, facilities get fewer and farther between, and the prospects of survival in the event of a forced landing or ditching more daunting.

"From September to June expect to encounter winter conditions like you've never seen before.

"If a member of your party shows any of these symptoms— uncontrollable fits of shivering; vague, slow, slurred speech; memory lapse; incoherence; immobile, fumbling hands; frequent stumbling; lurching gait; drowsiness; apparent exhaustion; and inability to get up after a rest—he is in trouble and needs your help.

"If you get the impression we feel that transatlantic flight is a foreboding undertaking for the uninitiated, you are correct."

I have heard more than one person say they thought anyone would have to be crazy to fly a single-engine plane across the ocean, whether you were twelve years old or fifty. If the single engine fails, you're in real trouble. I asked Curt if he would feel better flying a twin-engine plane.

"Why should I?" he replied. "That would only double the chances of engine failure." I thought that was pretty funny.

Vicki's Mother Corinne

"One time it was cold, windy, and rainy. Vicki was going to fly to Pittsburgh. I felt really guilty bringing her to the airport because I was afraid something terrible was going to happen. So I said to her, 'Vicki, does it scare you to fly in weather like this?' She just looked at me and said, 'Stop it! If it's raining you fly. If it's windy you fly. You fly! You can't be worried about flying.'"

My folks tried to scare me off the trip a little bit. My mom gave me a pamphlet with statistics on how many planes crashed trying to cross the Atlantic. It said seven planes went down over Greenland from 1986 to 1989 and that two people were killed. About two planes go down over Iceland every year. In 1987, two people crashed just a few miles short of the runway in Scotland. They were both killed.

She asked me if I'd considered the possibility that the plane could go down over the ocean.

"I think that would be neat," I replied. "It would be challenging to try and survive."

"Vicki, don't ever say that! You could *die!*"

"Mom," I explained, "different people have different opinions."

Vicki's Instructor, Curt Arnspiger

"Vicki tends to downplay danger. This is a trip that not many adults would attempt. It's intimidating for most people. She doesn't focus in on risks, which is good and bad. I don't know if she doesn't know enough to be afraid, or if she feels completely fearless. She hasn't had enough harrowing experiences to have the perspective of when to be afraid."

People ask me all the time if I get scared while I'm flying. Scared that the plane is going to go down. Scared that I'm going to die.

The answer is no. Never. It's out of the question. A true pilot just doesn't go into flying with that attitude.

Still, every pilot has to be prepared for all kinds of emergencies that might occur during a flight. And I was.

Even in warmer parts of the world, the ocean is pretty cold. Up in the North Atlantic, the water is very often below freezing (it doesn't turn to ice because of the salt). If you fall in that water, you become unconscious in minutes. You get hypothermia, which is when your body temperature falls so low that your organs can't function properly.

There wouldn't be any flotilla of ships escorting us across

the ocean, ready to rescue us. We had to be prepared in case it was necessary to ditch the plane and stay afloat until help arrived.

For this reason, Curt and I would have to wear immersion suits the entire trip. They looked sort of like scuba suits—red, rubbery, nearly ten pounds—and covered us

I did not dress up as Gumby for Halloween. This is the immersion suit I had to wear to fly across the Atlantic. I almost had to use it...

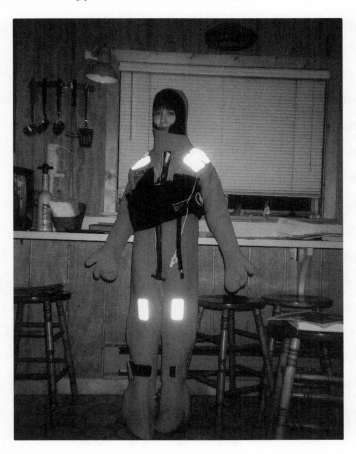

from head to toe. I looked really weird in mine, like I was dressed up as an alien for Halloween. Curt called me "the Michelin woman." It was uncomfortable to wear, too. But it would keep me warm and afloat for twenty-four hours, and that's what counts. I practiced swimming and floating in it before the trip.

Besides the immersion suits, we were required to have other things in the plane: two life jackets, a raft, water, food, a bail bucket, a mirror (for signaling planes, not to make yourself look pretty when they rescue you), a whistle, a knife, two flashlights, a fire extinguisher, a first-aid kit, a dye marker, a signaling sheet, a compass, sleeping bags, water-proof matches, a ball of string, a small stove, a saw (to cut through snow), candles, mosquito netting, insect repellent, and a survival at sea manual.

Even with all that stuff, you only have about a 50/50 chance of surviving until a rescue ship arrives to pick you up.

In reality, you have to hope your plane doesn't go down. Because if it hits the water it may sink immediately, and you won't be able to get all the supplies out anyway.

You may be wondering if we had parachutes. No, we didn't. Parachuting out of a plane makes sense if you get shot down over enemy territory during a war. It looks really good in the movies, too. But it doesn't make much sense otherwise.

When you parachute out of a plane, you lose control of the plane, of course. If you were flying over land, it might crash into somebody's house or a building full of people. You also destroy somebody's $30,000 plane. And if you parachute out and land in water, what are you going to do next?

It's much safer to glide the plane down as far as you can. Over land, you're supposed to put the plane down on a highway or field. Over water, you're supposed to skim it down to the surface, jump out as quickly as possible, and hop in the raft with your survival equipment.

There were two more pieces of equipment I needed for the flight, and Curt helped me get them. The first was a headset that had noise cancelling. It creates sounds in your ear that cancel out engine noise. That had bothered me a lot on the cross-country trip, and I didn't want to hear that ringing in my ears again.

The second piece of equipment is required on all transatlantic flights. It's called a GPS receiver, which stands for Global Positioning System. The system is made up of twenty-four satellites circling the earth twice daily, distributed in six orbits about 10,900 miles up in outer space.

These satellites transmit signals which are picked up by the GPS receiver.

The receiver is about the size of a Game Boy. You plug in where you took off and where you plan to land. The screen displays your exact location in latitude and longitude, how fast you are flying, and what direction, so that you don't get off course. It also displays the locations of airports around you. Your plane looks like a little **X** on the screen, and as you move the map moves with you. It's really cool.

Vicki's Brother Daniel

"When she told me she was going to fly across the Atlantic, I got scared. I didn't want anything to happen to her. Every time she went up I was afraid I'd never see her again. I'd say prayers for her and stuff."

As soon as word got out that I was going to fly the Atlantic, this nutty guy from New Jersey started calling my house. He tried to talk my dad into having me bring a *cat* along in the plane. According to this guy, Charles Lindbergh had a cat with *him* when he flew the Atlantic. Lindbergh was supposedly on the verge of falling asleep at the controls, when the cat rubbed against him and woke him up. The cat saved his life.

My dad told the guy that I would have a copilot with me

in case I started dozing off, but the guy wasn't satisfied. He kept calling my dad at home and at work, tracking us down wherever we were. He even called Curt to try and talk *him* into bringing a cat in the plane.

Eventually the guy stopped calling. I didn't think Monique or Lucy would have liked to fly across the Atlantic anyway.

Flying across the ocean involves more than carrying the right stuff in your plane. You have to train for it. Every Friday night for five weeks, my dad and I drove five hours to Columbus to work with Curt and two other pilots, Dick Willis and Mike Riley. Dick is an ex-Air Force pilot and Mike is a DC-10 captain who has been across the Atlantic seventy times in small planes. Both of them had taught Curt aspects of flying.

Curt, Mike, and Dick mainly taught me how to fly the Cessna 210. I had to get the feel of flying and landing the bigger plane. Most days I would land it fifteen or twenty times, until I really felt comfortable. Curt, Mike, and Dick also helped me fine-tune my flight plan and read the European maps.

Mike told me that around the same time I would be flying to Europe, he would be crossing the Atlantic in the opposite direction. He had been hired to ferry an old yellow World War II fighter plane back to the United States from Europe.

"Maybe we'll meet up somewhere in the middle," he said. It wasn't very likely because of the weather conditions and scheduling, but it would be fun to see him again overseas.

At the end of each of those training weekends, my dad and I drove back to Meadville so I could be ready for school on Monday morning.

On one of these weekends, Curt took me up in a jet plane he owns, a Spanish Saeta. He let me take the controls for a while and I flew it close to 300 miles per hour. Awesome!

The jet is controlled with a stick instead of a yoke, so you fly it with one hand. I did some flybys and it felt a lot different from the planes I was used to.

Curt told me he did some aerobatics and the jet could do some really steep turns.

"How steep?" I asked.

He took it into a sharp turn. I was pressed against my seat and felt like my flesh was going to rip away from my bones. Curt told me we were "pulling three Gs." One G is the average gravity on earth. When you experience two Gs, the force of gravity is twice as strong. At four and a half or five Gs most people black out.

All I can say is, I'll have to build my stomach up before I try pulling Gs in a jet plane again.

By May, I felt I was ready for the flight. The week before I was due to leave, our house was a madhouse. The phone didn't stop ringing all day. Radio stations from as far away as Australia, South Africa, and France were calling for interviews. NBC and CBS sent camera crews to Meadville, and they followed me and my family around all week.

I'd come home from school to find reporters hanging around the front porch and sitting in our living room. My mother was even barbecuing food for them. She and my dad were going crazy that week. I thought it was really exciting. I even got a letter from my friend Vice-President Al Gore, congratulating me for taking the trip.

Usually on the last day of the school year, we play volleyball and stuff. Anything but schoolwork! But NBC's *Dateline* came out to film me at school and my teacher Mrs. Dowler didn't want people to think we goof around all day. She wanted to conduct a math lesson, but we talked her out of it. *Dateline* ended up using about two seconds of a volleyball game.

My sixth grade graduation was held on June third. The next day I took off for Augusta.

I knew one thing for sure—writing an essay on "How I Spent My Summer Vacation" would be a breeze.

I thought we'd never get off the ground!

8

"The wings got me across the ocean and they'll get you over too."

Meadville, Pennsylvania: A year and a half earlier, I had seen the sign-up sheet for that first flight lesson at the Port Meadville Airport. Now I was taking off from that same airport for a trip across the Atlantic.

The runway was jammed with friends and press people from all over. There was a hot-air balloon on the airfield. As I answered questions, I noticed one of my teachers in the crowd, Mrs. Rusek. She was wearing a T-shirt that read, "I Was Vicki Van Meter's First Grade Teacher."

I was introduced to Gordon McConnell, a seventy-five-year-old man who had been a bomber pilot in World War II.

I asked Curt if he would feel safer if our plane had two engines instead of one.

In 1944 his B-24 was shot down over Austria. He parachuted out just as the plane was exploding. When Gordon hit the ground he was barely alive. The Germans took him prisoner.

While he was being moved from one prison camp to another, Gordon saw a group of German refugees get hit by an Allied bomber. The only survivor was an eleven-year-old girl. He protected her for two days until she reached her aunt's house.

Gordon told me I reminded him of that girl, and he pulled a set of silver wings out of his pocket. He told me he had worn them throughout the whole war.

The pre-flight inspection. You have to check everything. There have been cases of pilots finding birds' nests in their engines!

"The wings got me across the ocean," Gordon said, "and they'll get you over too." My mom pinned the wings on my flight suit.

A week earlier, I had been shopping with my folks and we stocked up on snacks for the trip. I brought along ten peanut butter Tiger's Milk bars, some energy bars, peaches, little boxes of Rice Krispies and Corn Pops, bottled water, and a bag of Cheetos. It wouldn't be as tasty as my mom's mashed potatoes and broccoli, but I knew there wouldn't be time to eat full course meals while I was flying.

Curt and I did the pre-flight inspection and we left Meadville at 11:00 A.M. As the plane lifted off the ground, I saw some of my friends standing on a hill near the runway. Before heading off, I dipped my wings to them. That's how pilots say hello or good-bye.

Augusta, Maine: We landed at Augusta State Airport at 2:30 P.M. We would be sleeping over in Augusta, so I had a little time for sightseeing before the trip.

I visited with a bunch of kids in a children's hospital and stopped off at the Samantha Smith memorial. Samantha Smith was an eleven-year-old Maine girl who wrote a letter to Russian President Yuri Andropov asking why he wanted to conquer the world. That was in 1983, before the Soviet Union split up, when the Cold War was still going on. Andropov invited her to visit the Soviet Union, and Samantha's mission of peace made her an international celebrity.

Two years later Samantha Smith, her dad, and six other people died when their small plane hit some trees and crashed twenty-five miles from Augusta. The memorial is a statue of a girl in blue jeans with her hands stretched out. There's a small bird on her shoulder.

Some newspaper articles compared me to Samantha Smith, but her goal was much more important than mine. Still, I hoped to take her spirit of goodwill with me across the ocean, and maybe continue in some small way what she had started.

The Samantha Smith memorial in Augusta.

I put some flowers next to the feet of Samantha's statue and said a prayer before leaving the memorial.

Sunday was a nice crisp day, a good day for flying. I put on my new blue flight suit, which I had received when I attended Space Camp. I slipped a small photo in one pocket, a picture of a six-year-old girl named Hallie Harmon. I had never met Hallie, but her mother heard about my trip and wrote me a letter asking if I would carry the photo across the ocean. She said it would be like Hallie was flying with me.

A high school band was playing when I got to the airport. Because I flew from Augusta on my cross-country trip, the town knew me and a lot of people were there to see me off. Press people from all over the world were crowding around. A tractor was wheeled out for me to stand on so the photographers would be able get their pictures.

Veda Grant, the eighty-year-old woman whom I'd met before the cross-country trip, came out to the airport again. She looked at Harmony and said, "I wish I could stow away in there."

Vicki's Flight Diary

"I loaded my stuff on the plane. Then I called to get weather and file the flight plan. The media followed me into the terminal. I wondered if we would ever get off the ground."

—Augusta, Maine

We got off the ground around noon. I circled the airport once, and as I was about to do a flyby Curt said, "Act like you're a fighter pilot." I took the plane down and dive-bombed over the crowd at 190 miles an hour. Then I dipped my wings and headed off. The coast of Maine grew smaller and smaller.

In Augusta, I dipped my wings at my friends and headed for Scotland.

Later, I would learn that many of the reporters wrote articles comparing me with Amelia Earhart. She was the first woman to fly across the Atlantic, and she took off just twenty miles from Augusta. Just like me, she became interested in flying when her dad took her to visit the opening of a new airfield (in Long Beach, California, in 1920).

Almost all the articles said I was flying the same route as Amelia, and some of them even said I took off on the same *date* she did so I could duplicate her journey.

That was a lot of nonsense. Amelia Earhart is one of my biggest heroes, but I wasn't following her route and I didn't leave on the same date. There was only one Amelia Earhart, and I would never want to take anything away from her accomplishments.

I guess I sort of look like Amelia Earhart, but something tells me that if I was a boy, nobody would have compared me with her.

Vicki's Flight Diary

"When we got the weather the man didn't acknowledge me and gave the weather to Curt . . ."

—Goose Bay, Canada

Goose Bay, Canada: Goose Bay is almost straight north and five and a half hours from Maine. I flew over the St. Lawrence Seaway, which was big and beautiful. Along the way to Goose Bay, I heard commercial airline pilots flying above us who were talking about me on the radio. They didn't know I was listening in on the same frequency.

"Hey, where's that little girl who's flying across the ocean?" they were saying.

"This is 127 Sierra, the girl who's flying across the ocean. Hi."

They greeted me back. Word was spreading about me, I

guess. One pilot told me he read about me in the paper that morning—and he was from the country of Jordan!

"Good landing," Curt told me after we hit the ground in Goose Bay at 5:30 P.M. "Any landing you can walk away from is a good landing." The sign outside the airport says "Happy Valley–Goose Bay."

Goose Bay is a jumping-off point for pilots and fur trappers. It's a tiny outpost in the middle of nowhere. When we arrived, there were no cameras or microphones. One person was on hand to greet us—the customs inspector. Commercial airlines don't fly to Goose Bay, so my parents weren't there. They had flown to Iceland, the next day's destination. I really missed them.

There *is* a hotel in Goose Bay. Actually two. But things weren't very lively there. In fact, it was really depressing. I was feeling pretty lonely and homesick. I was too embarrassed to ask Curt to keep me company, and I ate in my room by myself.

Vicki's Sister Elizabeth

"My parents couldn't be there at every stop and Vicki was all by herself in strange parts of the world. The night she stayed over in Goose Bay she called me from her hotel room.

She doesn't usually say, 'I love you guys' or anything like that. But she softened up and told me told me how lonely she was and how she really felt about me. She was starting to cry, and it broke my heart that I couldn't be there. I told her that I was with her, thinking about her, even if I wasn't in the room with her. And I told her I was very proud of her, that I believed in her, and I knew she could do it."

I had requested a wake-up call for 5:45 the next morning. When the phone rang, I said to myself that I'd just lay there for five more minutes before getting up. Naturally, I fell back asleep. Curt knocked on my door at 6:20 and asked if I was ready to go. I jumped out of bed, got dressed really quickly, and wolfed down some Corn Pops straight from the box.

It was chilly out, but not freezing. The cab driver who took us from the hotel to the airport said the temperature gets down to minus 40° every day during the winter.

This was the 50th anniversary of D-Day, the day the Allies stormed the beaches of Normandy, France to turn the tide of World War II. I wouldn't have anybody shooting at the plane, but I knew D-Day would be tough for me too. The next five-and-a-half-hour hop was going to be one of the hardest parts of the trip.

We would be heading east and north. The weather is

unpredictable in this part of the world. It can change very suddenly. That's not such a big problem for a jet because they fly so high in the sky. For small planes like ours, things can get dicey.

It takes twelve hours to fly from Goose Bay to Iceland, with a fuel stop in Narsarsuak (pronounced "Nar-sar-soo-ak"), Greenland. It was going to be an exhausting day. One hour of flying a plane, pilots say, feels like three or four hours of driving a car. You have to stay alert all the time.

The sky was filled with clouds, and we flew right through them at 8,900 feet over the water. We were a little over an hour into the flight when I glanced out the window and noticed we were picking up some ice on the wings. It wasn't raining outside, but when you fly through clouds in below freezing temperatures, moisture can accumulate on a plane and freeze.

Ice on the wings weighs a plane down and also changes the shape of the wing slightly so it doesn't fly as smoothly. Big commerical planes have de-icers, but small planes don't.

We weren't too worried at the time. A little ice on the wings in this part of the world is expected. I had chosen June for this flight specifically because the weather wouldn't be so bitter cold.

A few minutes later I looked out the window again, and I could see that the layer of ice on the wings was getting thicker. It was up to an inch or so. If we just kept going like that, the ice would become so heavy that the plane wouldn't be able to fly.

"This is really starting to build up," I said to Curt.

"Let's get on top of this stuff," he replied.

If we could climb above the clouds, the sun would melt the ice off the wings. But we kept climbing, and nothing happened, except we got more ice. After we climbed about 3300 feet, Curt said he could tell that we'd only have to climb about 100 feet more to get above the clouds.

I pulled back on the yoke, but the nose of the plane didn't go up, as it should. Not a foot.

We had waited too long. The wings had picked up so much ice that the plane was too heavy to climb. The engine just wasn't powerful enough.

It was becoming a very dangerous situation. At some point, there can be so much ice on the wings that the plane plunges right into the water. And if our flaps or other moving parts were to freeze up, we'd also be in real trouble.

Vicki's Instructor, Curt Arnspiger

*"If we continued at that altitude it would be poten-
tially . . . well, let's just say it would be an emergency. At the
rate we were picking up ice, we had maybe fifteen minutes to
get out of it."*

Curt and I didn't panic. We knew what we had to do. We had to get out of the clouds so we could stop picking up ice. And we had to do it in a hurry.

We thought about turning around and heading back to Goose Bay, but by this time we were halfway to Greenland, so we decided that we might as well keep going.

We had tried flying above the clouds, but the plane couldn't climb. There was no place to go but down.

Why would flying *below* the clouds melt the ice? For every thousand feet you go up in the air, the temperature drops three and a half degrees. That's true anywhere in the world.

So at 9,000 feet, the temperature is 31.5° colder than it is at sea level. If we dropped down below the clouds, the air would be much warmer, and hopefully it would melt the ice.

That is, of course, if we could get below the clouds.

I brought Harmony down to 7,000 feet and then 5,000 feet, but the air was still thick with clouds. We couldn't see the water at all. The ice on the wings was just as bad, if not worse.

I came down to 3,000 feet. Two thousand feet. Still the clouds were there and we still couldn't see the water.

Two thousand feet is really low. You don't want to fly *too* low over the ocean, because if you have an emergency and the plane goes down, there's no gliding time before you hit the water. You don't have time to radio for help or get out your raft and the other emergency gear.

Vicki's Instructor, Curt Arnspiger

"I was getting a bit nervous. You don't want to fly the plane into the ocean, obviously. We couldn't see the water and we weren't exactly sure how high over it we were. Our altimeter had been set 300 miles back, and the atmospheric pressure changes so the altimeter wasn't exactly accurate. It could have been off 500 feet one way or another. So when the altimeter read 2,000 feet, we could have been only 1,500 feet over the water. I told Vicki not to dive down. You just kind of gingerly feel your way down about 100 feet each minute, like a blind person making his way down an unfamiliar street with a cane to avoid bumping into things."

I brought Harmony down to 1,500 feet, and then 1,000 feet. We were *still* in the clouds. If the clouds went all the way down to sea level—which they do sometimes—there would be *no* way for us to get out of them. We couldn't go up, and we couldn't go down. And we were running out of time.

I don't even like to consider such possibilities, but at that moment there was a real danger we were going to crash.

*I snapped this picture between Goose Bay in Canada and Greenland.
There was no sign of life on the entire ice cap.*

Finally, at 800 feet over the water, we broke out from under the clouds. I breathed a sigh of relief, and I'm sure Curt did too. We kept going at 500 feet.

Flying so low, I could see the waves below me and birds skimming over the water. There were millions of chunks of ice, about the size of a raft, as far as the eye could see. It was a spectacular sight. In a few minutes, there was less ice on the wings and droplets of water were flying off them. Soon the ice was entirely gone. The crisis was past.

We were about eighty miles from Greenland, which is actually a province of Denmark. Icebergs started to appear in the distance. *Really* big icebergs. As we soared over them, I could see their white tips poking through the surface of the water. The rest of the iceberg, below the water and even more enormous, looked greenish.

Soon we could see the fjords of Greenland, long strips of land bordered by steep cliffs. I had to climb to 10,000 feet to clear the mountains. Without any ice on the wings, Harmony climbed easily. As we made our final approach, I could see a huge patch of white in the distance. If you overshoot the airport, I realized, you could end up on a *glacier*.

Narsarsuak, Greenland: I remembered from school that the Viking explorer Leif Erikson named it "Greenland" because he thought that would make people want to visit the island. That was pretty clever. In fact, Greenland is a cold, white, desolate place. You wouldn't want to spend your Christmas vacation there.

It's the world's largest island, but only about 54,000 people are hearty enough to live there. The entire population could fit into Yankee Stadium.

They charge five hundred dollars just to land at the airport in Narsarsuak. It closes at 5:00 P.M. and if you land later than that, they charge another hundred to open the airport for you. They also charge eight dollars a gallon for fuel.

No wonder hardly anybody lives in Greenland! It's the high cost of living! Curt told me he sometimes flies hours out of his way to avoid landing there.

Narsarsuak is at the southernmost tip of the island on the

From a distance, it looked like some sort of Inuit protest rally. Then I heard all these kids chanting my name.

map, but if you ask me it's in the middle of nowhere. The airport is one little strip of runway. A plane brings in supplies and leaves once every two weeks. Other than that, the town rarely gets visitors.

The people of Narsarsuak are Eskimos. They call themselves "Inuits," which means "people." There are only 170 Inuits in the whole town. I certainly wasn't expecting a welcoming committee in this part of the world.

But I was wrong. When I taxied off the runway, I was astonished to see about forty Inuit children and some of their parents. They were holding up signs and chanting. At first I thought they were having some kind of a protest rally. As we got closer, I could see the signs had my name on them. I could hear that the kids were chanting "Vicki . . . Vicki . . . Vicki!"

It was truly an awesome sight. We had studied the Inuits in school, and I wished I understood their language.

The kids all wanted my autograph. Instead of crowding around like American kids do, they stood in a perfect single-file line. That was pretty funny. The kids gave me a pin, a shirt, and a hat that said "Greenland" on it. One lady brought out her white husky dog. His name was Mickey, and he came over and licked my face.

A man who spoke English gave me flowers and asked, "Shall I take you to the cafeteria?" I thought he meant a small cafeteria in the airport, but instead he took us to the only restaurant in town. In the lobby was a giant sculpture of a polar bear.

They didn't have stuff like Coke or Pepsi or Sprite. They had pineapple and papaya pop and something called Jolly Cola. I would have liked to try some, but I didn't want to make my stomach upset. Instead, I had something even worse—a croissant with a layer of chocolate on top and cream on the bottom. It was delicious.

Back at the airport, the man who spoke English told me he wanted to show me something. He led me to a room.

"Look," he said, "We have TV!"

It was the only TV set in the whole town. That must be

how they knew I was coming. I saw how proud he was and pretended to be impressed. I didn't bother mentioning to him that some American homes have a TV in every *room*.

We spent about an hour in Narsarsuak before we took off for Iceland. It was another five-and-a-half-hour flight, flying mostly east and a little north. It had turned into a beautiful day, and the visibility was so good that I could see nearly fifty miles in front of me. There were no problems with ice. I was able to relax a little. Curt and I were both hungry, so we tore open the bag of Cheetos and munched on them. They turned our fingers orange.

The most amazing thing about this part of the trip is that we flew over an enormous icecap. It's a glacier two miles thick that covers 83 percent of Greenland. If the icecap were to melt for some reason, it would raise the water level all over the earth by twenty feet.

I looked out the window to see if I could spot any polar bear tracks. There was no form of life at all out there. Pretty awesome sight.

Reykjavik, Iceland: This would be as far north as we would reach. The island is about the size of Kentucky and less than 2,000 miles from the North Pole. We were almost at the top of the world.

Mountains surround Reykjavik (pronounced "rake-ya-

114

vik") Airport, which is on the southern part of the island. The mountains are actually volcanos, and one of them erupted a few years ago.

As we were coming into our final approach, I saw an old yellow plane on the runway. It took Curt and me a moment before we recognized it.

"Hey, Mike Riley's here!" I said. Riley was one of the pilots I trained with back in Ohio. I was really happy to see him. We touched down at around 9:00 P.M.

A NATO commander met the plane. It was great to see my parents again. "It's good to be here," Curt told everybody, "We've had a long day."

Vicki's Mother Corinne

"I was so worried, my nails were just about chewed off. The first thing Vicki said to us was 'Wow! We had such a great day! It was just fantastic!'"

I went out to a restaurant with my folks, Curt, and Mike, but I didn't eat much. I was never a really big meat eater, but in the last year I decided to stop eating meat entirely. Whenever I pick up a piece of meat I think of a cow or a chicken. I'd go drive down the road with my parents and see these animals and just not feel good about eating them. So now I'm a vegetarian.

In Iceland, about the only thing they have to eat is seafood. If somebody gave me a million dollars, I wouldn't eat fish. I ordered a salad, but it was really weird looking and I just picked at it.

Still, I had a great time that night. There I was in Iceland of all places, and I was surrounded by people who cared about me. It was a terrific feeling, especially after a very tough day.

Reykjavik is a real city with about 200,000 people. It isn't as cold as Greenland because the warm waters of the Gulf Stream go right by the island. In January, which is the coldest month, the temperature is about the same as it is in New York City.

It's interesting that Greenland has a lot of ice, while Iceland has a lot of green.

The strange thing about Iceland is that during the winter it's totally dark all day long. And in the middle of the summer, it never gets dark at *all*. This happens because the earth tilts to face the sun half the year and turns away from the sun the other half of the year. Iceland is very close to the North Pole, so the earth's tilt really affects it.

We checked into the Loftleidir Hotel and by the time we got to bed it was midnight. Outside, it looked like it was the middle of the day. It was really weird.

It felt better than great. It felt awesome.

9

"It's safer to suffer."

Curt and I left Reykjavik just before noon on Tuesday, June 7. This would be the last leg of the trip, a six-hour flight to Scotland.

Vicki's Flight Diary

"I was more comfortable in my survival suit than I was the other day. But it still wasn't silk pajamas."

—on the way to Glasgow

The first three hours were smooth, but then we found ourselves flying through clouds and I noticed ice forming on the wings.

Not again!

The last time we had an ice problem, I had waited too long to climb out of the clouds. I decided not to wait another minute this time. We were in radio contact with Scotland, so I requested clearance to fly higher. You have to get clearance, because there could be another plane flying in the area at that altitude.

This time, there was no problem climbing. I had to take Harmony all the way up to 13,500 feet before we popped out of the top of the clouds and the sun began to melt the ice. I could hardly see the ocean. Once in a while there would be a small hole in a cloud and I'd see the water through it.

Just as it's risky flying too low, it's also risky flying very high. The atmosphere surrounding the earth becomes thinner the higher you go. If you fly above 12,500 feet, pilots are supposed to either come back down or breathe oxygen every half hour. Jet airplanes are pressurized, which means they pump oxygen in continuously so you don't realize how thin the air is up there.

We never expected to have to fly that high for so long, and we didn't bring an oxygen tank with us. There was no room in the plane for it anyway. But I really wished we had one.

Curt had been up in thin air many times before and he

118

was used to it. Even so, he told me he had a headache. I'm much smaller than him of course, and my body was having a harder time due to the lack of oxygen. I felt very tired suddenly, and found myself gasping for breath.

There was nothing we could do about it. It was either stay up there in the thin air and suffer, or fly lower and risk ice forming on the wings again. We decided it would be safer to suffer.

We were still an hour and a half from Scotland. I felt my eyes rolling back in my head and had to force myself to concentrate. I thought I was going to pass out any minute. I was really pushing my body to its limit. I did my best not to let Curt see how much I was suffering.

In everyday life, we take the air we breathe completely for granted. Flying where the air is so thin, I came to appreciate how important it is to our bodies.

I had just about reached my limit when the coast of Scotland appeared in the distance. Gratefully, I brought the plane down to a more reasonable altitude and gulped air.

Scotland is just north of England. When we broke through the clouds, it looked a little bit like the Rocky Mountains. Then it started to get more green and rolling. We passed over some big islands before Glasgow control came over the radio.

Vicki's Flight Diary

"I was hungry and thirsty. I ate some but did not drink because this was the longest flight without stops and I didn't want to take chances if you know what I mean. I was pretty thirsty, though."

—on the way to Glasgow

Glasgow, Scotland: It was a bright and sunny day, but very windy. As I approached the runway at Glasgow International Airport, the controller asked me to switch to another, smaller runway because of the wind.

I was concerned because I had learned to land on pretty big runways. It's a lot tougher when you don't have as much room to land on. Luckily, there were nineteen knots of headwind on the smaller runway. Headwind slows a plane down quite a bit, so it makes a small runway feel like a bigger one.

There were tough crosswinds too. The landing was okay. I didn't bounce the plane or anything like that. We hit the tarmac at 6:30 P.M.

"Congratulations, 127 Sierra," said the controller.

It was over. Six months earlier I had set a goal to fly a plane across the Atlantic Ocean, and I had done it. It felt great. Better than great. It felt awesome.

Curt tried to drench me, but most of the champagne landed on him. Gotta watch out for those crosswinds.

I pulled off my immersion suit as soon as I got out of the plane and put on a pair of sneakers. My parents' plane was due to arrive in Scotland a few hours later.

Somebody handed us a bottle of champagne. Curt shook it up, popped the cork, and squirted it toward me. Unfortunately for him, he didn't allow for those crosswinds, and the champagne blew all over him. He didn't seem to mind.

I didn't drink any champagne, but Curt took a few gulps. He seemed a little happier than usual as we met the press.

The foreign reporters were even more aggressive than Americans. They were elbowing each other out of the way to get their questions in. I told them about the problems we had with the ice and the altitude, but I didn't let on how tough the trip had been.

I told one little lie, saying we had dropped as low as 1,000 feet over the water to get out from under the clouds. If I told them we were actually just 500 feet over the water, I'm sure people would have been alarmed at how dangerous the situation had been.

"I always thought it would be real hard," I admitted truthfully, "and it was."

The European Tour.

10
Two final tasks

My mission across the Atlantic was accomplished, but I had two small chores to do while I was in Europe. For the first one, Curt and I flew to London. We landed at Biggen Hill, which was a big fighter-plane base during World War II.

Before I'd left the United States, some schoolchildren in Somerville, Maine, had given me an envelope with a red ribbon on it. They asked if I could deliver it to a man named Richard Branson in England.

In 1987, Branson crossed the Atlantic in a hot air balloon. He is also a billionaire who owns Virgin Airlines and Virgin Records.

Biggen Hill was the fighter-plane base the Allies used during World War II.

I had no idea how I was going to get in touch with Richard Branson, but it turned out I didn't have to. The story of my flight had been all over the news, and word got to Branson that I had a letter for him. Branson found out what hotel I was staying at with my parents.

I was taking a shower when a man called our room from the lobby. My father picked up the phone. "Hello," the voice said, "This is Richard Branson, and I was wondering if Vicki and her family might join me for toast and tea."

I never showered so fast in my life.

I gave Mr. Branson the letter, and he was totally charming. He said he hoped we could travel to Mars together someday. He also invited my family to visit his home, but unfortunately we couldn't go. I had that second chore I had promised to complete.

Vicki's Flight Diary

"We went over the ocean so the BBC could get their photos. It was a cloudy day and the bottoms were low. Once in a while there would be a big cumulus cloud and we would go through and bounce but then we would pop out. I had to pick up a clearance to climb up to 9,000 feet. In the meantime I was circling around and dodging clouds."

—London

There's a little town north and east of Paris, France, called Fismes (pronounced "feem"). In World War I, some Meadville soldiers helped liberate the town. During World War II food was scarce in Fismes, and Meadville sent a boxcar filled with food to help out.

1994 was the 50th anniversary of Fismes' liberation from the Nazis, so the Meadville City Council made a plaque to commemorate the longstanding friendship between the two cities. Because I was flying across the Atlantic, they asked me if I would make a side trip to Fismes and formally present the plaque. I said I would be glad to.

This plaque was placed on a bridge in Fismes, France, to honor the friendship with my hometown in Pennsylvania.

There are two runways at Prunay airport outside of Fismes. One is paved, but it's very narrow and only 3,000 feet long. I was used to the 10,000 foot runways back home. The other runway is grass. That one isn't much longer, but grass slows down a plane more quickly.

I asked for permission to put Harmony down on the grass runway. I had practiced landing on grass many times at Rust Field back home in Pennsylvania, so it was a piece of cake. We kicked up a lot of dust when we touched down.

Fismes must really love Meadville. They even named a street in the town "Rue de Meadville." Only 5,000 people live in Fismes, but it seemed like all of them came out to greet me. They had a marching band and parade. Everyone wanted to give us dinner, so we ate for about eight hours straight. Fismes is right in the middle of champagne country, and Curt, my parents and I were taken on a tour of a champagne factory.

I presented the plaque to the mayor of Fismes and made a short speech about the friendship between the people of Meadville and the people of Fismes. It was fascinating to hear my words translated into French a second after I spoke them. The plaque was put on a bridge, where it will be as long as that bridge is standing.

Some of the soldiers who had fought in World War II were in the crowd. My dad said some of them had tears in their eyes, but I didn't see that.

While I was in Fismes, we met a family who had a son my age named Sebastian. He couldn't understand English very well and I don't know any French at all, but he had a video game system and we had fun playing together. We were able to talk a little bit about "Sonic the Hedgehog" and stuff like that. It was nice to hang around with a kid for a change.

At one point Sebastian said to me, "I play soccer with my rabbit." I said, "Yeah, sure," figuring I had misunderstood what he was trying to tell me. But then Sebastian led me outside and showed me this bunny he called Poupon. He threw a soccer ball toward Poupon, who dashed after it and

Poupon playing soccer.

started kicking it around the backyard. It was pretty amazing. Too bad they don't have "Stupid Pet Tricks" in France.

During dinner Poupon got a little too friendly with the soccer ball, but I won't go into that.

There's no place like home.

11

"So what are you going to do next?"

That summer had been different from all other summers in my life. After the trip across the Atlantic, I was invited on all the talk shows again and got to meet lots of celebrities. Sometimes people recognized me on the street and treated *me* like a celebrity.

It was exciting, but I didn't think I got much of a real summer vacation of going to the pool and hanging out with my friends. I would be home for a couple of days, and then I would have to go somewhere.

One time I was in the lobby of a New York hotel when I saw a guy who looked really familiar. I stared at him for a few moments and suddenly realized he was Hulk Hogan, the wrestler. Before I could go over and get his autograph, he came over to me and said, "Hey Vicki, I saw you on TV. How was the flight?" That was really neat.

Then a few weeks later, I was in California waiting in the dressing room at *The John and Leeza Show*, and who should walk in but Hulk Hogan. "Is that you?" he said. "Who's following who around?"

The thing that really felt great—much more than being on TV and meeting famous people—was receiving letters from kids all around the world. I wish I could print all their wonderful messages, but I'll share just a few.

One of the nicest things that happened to me was receiving letters from kids all over the world.

Dear Vicki,

I think it was cool to fly all that way. It was very brave and I think that's one leap for kid kind. I hope more kids will try to follow in your footsteps.

Your friend,

Patrick Langer

Dear Vicki,

At school we have goals, and I have made a lot of them. When I heard about your flight it really made me think about what I can do and what I can accomplish. I think it's really cool that you would like to be the first woman to go to the moon! I hope you are.

Rachel

Naturally, as soon as I flew across the Atlantic everybody started asking me what I'm going to do *next*.

Right now, I'm happy to be a typical American teenager: going to school, playing video games, watching TV, going to the movies, taking tennis lessons, and doing normal kid stuff. I'm not bored at all.

Visiting kids in children's hospitals has given me a really good feeling, and I'd like to do more of that. I want to learn to speak other languages too, because we Americans are not the only people in the world.

Once a month or so, I hope to fly. It's not like riding a bike. If you go too long without flying, you lose your skills. I want to get my pilot's license when I turn sixteen so I can fly solo. *Pilot's* license? I'd like to get my *driver's* license. It's sort of funny that I flew a plane across the Atlantic Ocean, but I can't drive my dad's minivan around the corner to go to the store.

I want to learn to fly gliders and low wing planes, do aerobatics, and formation flying. I'll probably go through instrument flight school, where you learn to fly when you can't *see* anything.

I'll graduate from regular high school in the year 2000. Down the road, I hope to attend the Naval Academy, and maybe work for NASA.

Who knows, maybe I'll follow my original dream and become an astronaut. A man from NASA visited my school once and told our class that by the time we're old enough to be astronauts, NASA will be ready to send someone to Mars.

That would be really cool—to be the first Earthling to set foot on another planet.

But I'm keeping my options open. Maybe my interests will change over the next few years. Lately I've been thinking that it might be interesting to become an archaeologist or a lawyer. Whatever I decide to do, I'm going to give it all I've got.

I may never have the opportunity to meet another celebrity or be on TV again, and that's okay. As I've said, I never became a pilot to become famous. I became a pilot because I love to fly. I enjoy setting goals and achieving them.

You don't have to fly across an ocean or be on TV to prove to yourself that you can do something good. It can be an art contest or a running race or anything else that's important to you.

When I was younger, I never thought I would do anything like fly a plane. But I decided I wanted to do it, so I did it. And achieving that goal has given me more confidence in sports, getting good grades in school, and dealing with people. Any kid can do the same thing, whatever you put your mind to. You don't have to be a boy, or a girl, or a black or a white person.

Whatever your goal, there will always be obstacles thrown in your path. Racism, sexism, ageism, whatever. I remember I was in third grade and they were passing out applications for the Little League. When I went to sign up, I was told that girls played in the softball league and boys played in the baseball league.

I don't like softball. So I said, "If I can't play baseball, I'm not going to play."

I guess they were afraid my family would sue or something, so they agreed to give me a tryout. A coach threw me a pop fly, a line drive, and ground ball. When the tryout was finished and the coaches picked their teams, I was selected in the first round.

That felt great! When you achieve your goal after somebody says you don't even have the right to *set* that goal, that makes the achievement even much more rewarding.

There's nothing that says a kid can't have a philosophy about life, and here's mine: The secret of success can be summed up in one word—try. Don't worry about what you *can't* do—find out what you *can* do and try your hardest to develop that.

I came across an old African saying in a book one day, and it really made me think . . .

If you can walk, you can dance.
If you can talk, you can sing.

I added one more line to that poem . . .

If you can dream, you can do anything.